Visitor's Guide to London

Copyright © 2015.

By
Blair Howard

Ok, so when I set out to write this guide for visitors to London I ran into a problem, a large problem: there are literally 1,001, more even, things to see and do in England's capital city, many of them obscure and off the beaten path. A complete guide to the city of London would take up a couple of thousand pages, at least. So what to do?

It took a little thought, but I think I found the answer. Most visitors to London have only a week, or two, to visit and view the best that this great city has to offer. Some visitors come with some preconceived ideas of they want to see and do. Most do not. It seemed to me, then, that most visitors will want to visit the major sites and attractions. To visit London and not see them would, I think, create something of void. It would be a shame to have to say, "No, I never did manage to get to…."

This guide book, then, is devoted to London's major attractions, and a few not so major attractions that I think most visitors would be pleased to see. I have also included one or two day trips out of the city; most visitors find they need a bit of a break after several days of walking the city. Thus you'll find detailed itineraries for day trips to Shakespeare Country (including Stratford upon Avon, and Warwick and Kenilworth castles); Stonehenge; and finally a quick look at the English Cotswolds. Depending upon how much time you have available, you can do one or all of them.

You'll also find a lot of practical information: how to get around the city, where to stay, and so on and so forth. My plan was to provide you with, not a definitive reference guide, but one that will serve you well during what for most people is the holiday or vacation of lifetime. Enjoy your visit to what is arguably the greatest city in the world.

Table of Contents

First, as I have already mentioned, this book is not intended to be the definitive guide to London. It is a guide for visitors to the city: folks with just a few days or perhaps a couple of weeks that want to see the sights, enjoy a good meal, find a nice place to stay, and figure out how to easily get around the great city. Within these pages you will find all of that, plus a lot more, all of it designed to make your visit both memorable and enjoyable.

London is, at least to me, the eternal city. Its history goes back more than two thousand years. Londinium was established as a Roman town in AD43, but there is evidence of settlement way back into the bronze and prehistoric ages. And the city has been England's capital for more than 1,000 years – although it's not known exactly when it achieved that status. For sure, London had been the capital during the reign of King Edward the Confessor (1042-1066), and perhaps even as far back as 100AD when Londinium superseded Colchester as the Roman capital of the province. When the Normans arrived in England in 1066, they established the capital at Winchester. It is thought, although no one can agree on a precise date, that government returned to London in the mid-12th century.

Okay, that's enough history, at least for now. It's not my intention to bore you. If you want to know about London's history, there are plenty of places online to find it.

My own love affair with England's first city began when I was a child. My mother and I would make day trips, on the train, to London. Sometimes to shop, sometimes to go sightseeing, and sometimes just to spend a pleasant hour or two walking the river banks. Later in life, I spent a lot of time in the city - job related –and then as a travel writer. I moved to the United States some years ago, but that did not mean an end to my relationship with London. I visit regularly and I stay on top of what's going on and what's new.

London is all things to all people, a great cosmopolitan gathering of just about every nationality in the world. Because of its long and checkered history, there is no city on earth with more to see and do than London: vast museums, ancient buildings, grand churches and cathedrals, beautiful parks and public gardens and, of course, the great and ever-present river Thames that dominates it.

Tower Bridge – Courtesy of Creative Commons and Tony Hisgett

I had several reasons for writing this book, not least of which was to share my love of London with you. More than that, though, I was unable to find a guide book that wasn't "dry" and uninteresting; they certainly weren't much help to visitors to London.

This book is different. You will find what you need to make your trip to London a memorable success. I have included all the top attractions, some with fees and some free. I've provided some ideas of where to stay, mostly those hotels of which I have personal experience. And I have provided enough of the practical information you will need to live for a couple of weeks or so within the city. I have also provided you with itineraries for several day trips outside the city, just the ones I think you'll enjoy, trips I often take myself, even though I have taken them countless times already; they never get old and I know you will enjoy them too.

Throughout the book I have included a large number of photographs – some to illustrate key points, some just for my own enjoyment, and for yours, I hope. I have also included some maps to help you find your way around, and to help with planning your itinerary. Enjoy!

Visas:

As of this writing, if you are a citizen of Australia, Canada, New Zealand, South Africa or the USA, you need a valid passport and will receive at your point of entry, 'leave to enter' the UK for up to six months. You will not be allowed to work in the UK unless you have a work permit. Citizen of the EU do not need a visa to enter the UK; they are also free to stay/live for as long as they like, and may work if they wish too.

UK Customs:

If you arrive in the UK from any country outside EU (European Union), you will have to comply with the UK Customs regulations. Countries belonging to the EU operate a "two-tier" customs system: one for duty free goods purchased outside the EU, and one for those purchased within the EU where the taxes and duties are paid at the point of purchase.

Visitors arriving from countries outside the EU are allowed to import:

- Tobacco: you may import 200 cigarettes or 50 cigars or 250g of tobacco, or any combination thereof.
- Alcohol: you may import 4 liters of non-carbonated wine *plus* 1 liter of spirits over 22% proof, OR 2 more liters of wine (sparkling wine if you like), and again you make up your alcohol allowance from any combination of alcohol products.
- Perfumes: there are no restrictions.
- Beer: the allowance is 16 liters of beer
- Electronics, Cameras and Souvenirs and other duty-free goods to the value of £300.

If you are arriving in the UK from an EU country, you can bring in a limited amount of duty-paid goods. Depending upon your country of origin, those goods may cost less than you would pay for them in the UK. Imported duty-paid items are deemed to be for "individual consumption," and that means there are limits to how much you can import into the UK:

- 800 cigarettes
- 200 cigars
- 1 kilo of tobacco
- 10 liters of spirits
- 20 liters of fortified wine (port, sherry etc.)
- 90 liters of wine, including no more than 60 liters of sparkling wine (Champagne etc.)
- 110 liters of beer

And, of course, there are a number of items banned by the UK Customs Service:

- Illegal drugs (cocaine, marijuana, heroin, morphine, etc.)
- Weapons (guns, flick knives, knuckledusters, swords, etc.)
- Pornographic material - other than that can legally be purchased in the UK
- Counterfeit goods and goods that infringe patents (handbags, watches, DVDs, CDs, etc.)
- Meat, milk and other animal products.

Staying in Touch – Using Your Smartphone

If you're planning a trip to London, staying in touch with the folks back home, planning your route, accessing the web, and so on and so forth, is an important consideration. That being so, the smart phone, and most of us have them these days, would seem to be the answer. Almost all smartphones will work in the UK, once you've activated your account to allow international access, that is.

You'll be able to make calls, send text, access the web, map your routes, and use your favorite apps. Unfortunately, all of which can be very expensive.

American smartphone users rarely think about the cost of roaming, data usage and such. Most of their packages come with virtually unlimited minutes and data. This is not the way it is when you travel abroad. When you place a call within the EU, your provider must connect to a local carrier to make the connection, and that comes with a cost. So... what to do?

Call your carrier and discuss your options and purchase an international plan for phone calls.

Without such a special plan, both AT&T and Verizon charge high per-minute rates: Verizon charges $1.29 per minute for calls you make or receive while in the UK. You can purchase Verizon's international calling plan for $4.99 per month which will reduce the cost to a little more manageable 99 cents per month; a similar plan offered by AT&T costs $5.99 per month – better, but still not cheap. Both plans allow you to check your emails.

Both Verizon and AT&T offer special data plans; you'll need one of those too. Verizon charges a base rate of $20.48 for one megabyte of data, but you can purchase data in 100 megabyte packages for $25 (overages cost $25 per 100MB); seems a silly not to do so.

If you don't plan on using data while traveling, go to "settings" in your device and turn Data Services off.

And speaking of that, you should always turn off your phone when you're not using it. If your phone rings while you're in the UK, you will be charged by the minute, even if you don't answer it.

Dialing the U.S.

Dial the Plus Sign (+) then 1 then enter ten digit U.S. number

Mapping Your Route

Mapping your routes comes out of your data package, so you'll need to be very careful; you also need to be remember that while you're are using the mapping software, your phone is on and can receive calls, for which you will be charged even if you don't answer them (1 minute minimum).

Texting: Texting today is more popular than making a call. Verizon does not have a special plan for texting; they charge $.50 to send and $.05 to receive a text message in the EU. No special plans or deals. AT&T's plan is a little different. Without their international texting plan, you will be charged $.50 to send a text, but that can drop as little as $.10 each if you purchase their $50 international texting plan - 500 text messages.

Pay as You Go Mobile Phones

Pay as you go is a terrific option for visitors to the EU. I used this option on my last visit to Paris. I simply purchased a SIM card for my phone: not a smartphone, just a regular Blackberry. There are no specific plans for the pay as you go option, you simply buy credit from phone centers of newsagents with 'Top-Up' signs in their windows.

Check with your phone company and find out which UK SIM cards will work in your phone. UK SIM cards cost £5-£10. If your phone is not compatible, no problem: you can purchase a pay as you go phone in the UK for £50 to£100 each. Mobile phone companies in the UK are: T-Mobile, Virgin Mobile, and Vodaphone. These are the premier providers, but there are others. The cost of mobile calls varies according to the provider; text messages within the UK cost about 10p.

About Money

The UK unit of currency is the pound sterling (£), often called a "quid" by the locals, thus something that costs £2 would be a couple of quid, in local terms.

At the time of writing, the Pound is worth $1.66 U.S. Yes, you will get £1 for each $1.66 you exchange, but don't let that fool you. On my many journeys home to the UK, I have found that what might cost $1 in the U.S. might well cost £1 in the UK. Thus the cost of many goods and goodies in the UK can be confusing. Also, do not fall into the trap, as many foreigners do, of thinking £1 = $1. You will soon run out of funds if you do.

Currency Exchange

It's never been easier to change your money into UK pounds, and the costs to exchange it have never been more wide ranging. You can change your money many different sources, at home and in London. These would include airports, banks, travel agencies and street kiosks, all of them in business to make a profit. Always check the current rate of exchange before you make a deal. The best rates are usually available at local banks; the worst rates are at the airport (very tempting), the currency exchange kiosks in the city, and at the railway stations. I usually exchange some of my dollars at my local bank in the U.S. before leaving the states. This gives me a good rate and some ready cash for bus, Tube and taxi fares, and snacks, when I arrive in London. Then I make a bigger buy at one of the banks, such a Lloyds or Barclays.

Traveler's Checks:

Traveler's checks are the best and safest way to carry your money. I take most of my cash in the form of traveler's checks, almost always purchased from American Express, mainly because of the worldwide support and availability of local Amex offices in London and other major cities.

Always buy your traveler's checks in UK pounds. If not, you'll be required to pay exchange fees when you change them in London.

Credit and Debit Cards

Credit cards, and most debit cards, are universally accepted in the UK. But you will need some cash as well, to pay for snacks, coffees, and the Tube (London's Underground Railway system). Use your credit cards to pay for large items, hotels, eating out, car rentals etc., and use your debit card to get the cash you need at an ATM machine (see below) That way, you'll always get the best rate of exchange, and you won't need to carry around large amounts of cash.

ATM Machines:

Personally, I have never had a problem finding an ATM machine in London, or elsewhere in the UK. If you have to ask for directions to the nearest ATM, you will need to remember to ask for a 'cash machine' or a 'cash point.' I tend to rely heavily on my debit card, not only is it quick and easy, you'll get the best rate of exchange when the charges get back to own bank.

Getting Around:

I have spent time in many of the major cities of the world, including New York, Washington, Los Angeles, Paris and so on, but I have never found a city where getting around is easier than London. I can, literally, move from one section of the city in a matter of minutes, or I can take as long as I like. The London Public Transport System is like no other in the world. I use the Tube almost exclusively, the London Bus System sometimes, and the London taxies only when I have to.

The Oyster Card:

I highly recommend you get one of these as soon as you arrive in the city. The Oyster Card is a plastic card, much like a credit card, with a cash balance that you can easily add extra cash to at newsagents and Tube and train stations, that you can use Tube or the bus fares. You save money because it's cheaper than paying cash. It's also a lot easier to use than paying cash: you simply touch the card to the yellow reader at the Tube station or on the bus; the reader then beeps to indicate that the fare has been deducted.

One more thing, don't be tempted to dodge the fare; ticket inspectors are everywhere, and they have readers that can read your card and they will know if you have paid, or not. If you haven't paid, you will be removed and slapped with an instant £10 fine.

The yellow card readers are at the front of all London buses, and at the turnstiles at all Tube stations; you'll need to scan your card to enter and exit each station.

Oyster cards can be purchased at newsagents, at Tube and train stations, and online at oyster.tfl.gov.uk.

As it is so easy, I strongly recommend using the Oyster Card on your next visit to London.

The Tube:

The London underground train network, most commonly referred to as the Tube, or even the Underground, is arguably the most user-friendly public transport system in the world. It is a network of underground routes covering the entire city, and then some. These routes are commonly called "lines." Each line, and there are 12 of them, are color-coded: the Piccadilly line is coded dark blue, the Victoria line is light blue, the metropolitan line is plum colored, and so on. The system can be a little confusing at first but, if you take a little time to study the map, you'll quickly get the hang of it.

Map: London Tube System

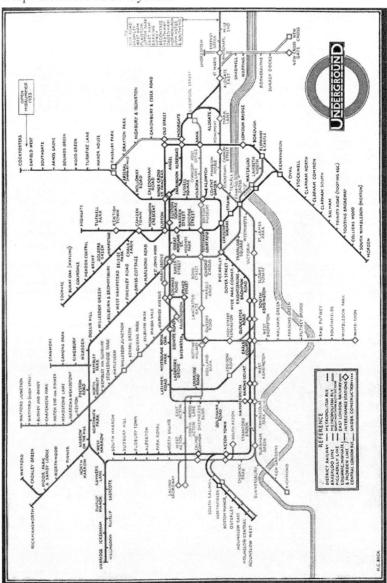

Map Courtesy of Creative Commons

The Tube is the quickest, easiest, and most convenient way to get around the city; it's also a lot of fun. You can be anywhere you like within a matter of just minutes. Trains run every couple of minutes during peak hours, and about every five minutes thereafter.

The Tube is not a 24-hour system. During the week, service begins around 5am starting from the ends of the lines and thus reach the more central stations around 5.30-6am. On Sundays, the Tubes begin around 7am. Service ends between 11:30pm and 12:30am, depending upon the location, meaning the last trains leave the central stations at 11:30, or thereabouts; **be sure to check the time of the last train you need; never assume anything.**

The Platform at Heathrow Tube Station. Not very appealing, but serviceable. If you're arriving in London at Heathrow, the Tube will get you where you need to go, fast - Photo Courtesy of Creative Commons.

There are some 275 Tube stations, more than 60 of which are in central London. You'll find that there is a Tube station serving all of the major attractions, shops, museums, parks and a whole lot more. You'll also find that, in central London, there is a Tube station within a short walk, no matter where you might be.

If you're staying outside of London, it makes sense to drive to one of the outlying stations, park the car, then take the Tube into and around the city. For instance, when I am staying at home, I usually park my car at White City and take the Tube into the city from there (the trains are above ground outside the city).

A Typical Tube Station Entrance – **Photo Courtesy of Creative Commons and Caroline Ford**

One more thing: ALWAYS stand on the right when using the escalators up and down to the Tube station; nothing makes a Londoner angrier than people standing on the left and blocking the way, especially when they are in a hurry; and they always are in a hurry.

Pay for Tube travel using the Oyster Card, it's much cheaper in the long run.

How to Use the Tube:

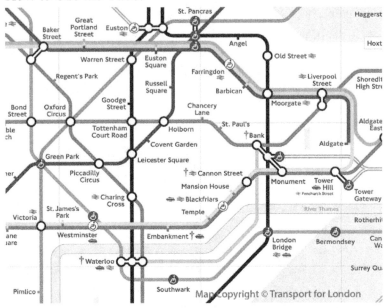

Using the Tube is really easy, provided you know what you're doing, which is why I rarely use any other form of transport when I'm in London. Here's how to do it:

First, let's look at the very small section of the Tube lines map you see above. It has some stops and stations we are particularly interested in, so it's a good example:

As you can see, all of the lines are colored. Below is a list of the tube lines and their colors.

The first thing we need to do is identify exactly where we want to go to, and from where.

So, let's suppose we want to go shopping on Oxford Street and we are at our hotel on Belgrave Road in Waterloo. We know that our nearest Tube station is Victoria, so we take out our map of the Tube, and we see that Waterloo station is at the intersection of three lines: Jubilee (Grey), Northern (Black) and the Bakerloo Line (Brown). We can also see that the Oxford Circus Tube station is on the Bakerloo line.

So, looking at the map, we can see we need to get on a tube train on the Bakerloo line and go several stops to Oxford Circus; it's just that easy. Ok, suppose we've had enough shopping and would like to see the Houses of parliament in Westminster. We can see that Westminster and the Embankment are on the District and Circle Lines (Yellow and Green). We need to get on a train somewhere on Oxford Street on the Central (Red) line, and head back to Oxford Circus, change trains to the Victoria (Light Blue) line and go to Victoria Station and then change trains to either the District or Circle lines and head to either the Westminster or Embankment stations.

Complicated? Nah, you'll soon get the hang of it.

London Buses

Photo of a London Double Decker Bus – Courtesy of Creative Commons

The London buses are another way to get around the city quickly and easily. Personally, I use them only rarely, preferring instead to use the Tube. But that's just me. The London double-decker bus is the ideal vehicle for sightseeing around the city. And it's easy enough to hop on and off at the main bus stops in the city center. Speaking of which, there are two types of bus stops: main stops and request stops.

Bus Stops

Main Bus Stops: all buses stop at all main stops. Main stops are signified by a plain white sign with a red London Transport symbol and the number of the bus routes it serves – see next page.

A Main Bust Stop Sign – Courtesy of Creative Commons

Request Bus Stops

Buses do not stop automatically at request stops; yes, you have to request the driver to make the stop. If you're at the stop, you have to stick your arm out to 'hail' the bus as it approaches; if you're on board, you will need to reach up and rind the bell: be sure to give the driver plenty of notice. Request bus stops signs are only little different from main ones: only the word "Request" has been added.

I'm not providing a map of the London bus routes, because the system is vast, buses are always available everywhere and almost all of the time.

Pay for your bus ride with your Oyster Card, you'll save a bunch of time and money in the long run.

A Request Bus Stop Sign – Courtesy of Creative Commons

My advice: use the buses for sightseeing and for quick, short trips around the city center. Use the Tube for longer trips.

London Taxis

Ah, the good old London Black Taxi is something of an icon around the city. Personally, I use them only in an emergency. They are expensive.

If you do need to use a taxi, you can have your hotel call one for you or, if you are out and about, simply hail one just as you would back home.

Cabwise:

If you do need a taxi in a hurry, use Cabwise. You can text CAB to Cabwise at 60835 and you will immediately receive a return text with the numbers to two local licensed minicab companies. This is a good option if you are out to dinner and need a quick and easy way back to your hotel; make the call about 10 minutes, or so, before you need the service.

A Word of Warning

Only the black London taxis can pick up customers on the street. Minicabs cannot. It is illegal for a minicab driver to pick up passengers on the street.

If a minicab driver approaches you, refuse the offer. There is a very good reason why you should not allow any vehicle other than the black London taxi to pick you up; it is, as the English say, "bloody dangerous."

All minicab rides must be booked directly through their companies: use Cabwise to get numbers – text CAB to 60835.

Things to Do
How Much Does it all Cost?

There are more things to see and do in and around London than you can possibly imagine, some of them free, some of them require an entrance fee, some of those are fairly inexpensive and some are quite expensive. Sightseeing in London is not cheap. There are, in fact, more than enough free attractions in and around the city for you to be able to spend your days sightseeing and not spend a penny, except for fares and such, but then you will miss many of London's top attractions; something you may not wish to do. That being so, I've provided a mix of free and fee-based attractions that I think are the essential, must visits.

As you peruse the listing below, you'll find I've also provided the cost of visiting the attractions, free or fee based.

If they are fee based, it's a good idea to see if you can book in advance, online or by telephone. You might be able to save a little money if you do; where the online option is available, I have provided the web address for you.

Then, of course, there is the much vaunted London Pass.

The London Pass

The London Pass offers free admission to more than 60 attractions in and around the city, including most of the "must-see" attractions: historic buildings, and including the Tower of London, Westminster Abbey, St. Paul's cathedral, even Windsor Castle, and so on; and it's accepted for a variety of tours, cruises and walks. You can definitely save money on admissions with the London Pass; in addition, you'll find there are a number of other advantage to the Pass, it's convenient and will save you time that would otherwise be spent standing in line. To make the most of it, however, you'll need to do some serious planning ahead, make a list of things you want to see and do, then weigh the pros and cons as to whether or not the pass will save you time and money.

Your London Pass will be valid for 12 months from the date of purchase so it makes good sense to buy early and plan wisely.

At the time of writing, a one-day adult pass costs £47 ($78); a one-day child pass – age 5 to 15 - is £30 ($50)

For two-day passes, adults pay £64 ($106) and children £47 ($78)

For three-day passes the cost is £77 ($128) for adults and £53 ($88) for children.

The six-day passes are £102 ($170) for adults and £72 ($120) for children.

For purposes of purchase, children are defined as travelers between the ages of 5-15.

The prices listed above were current at the time of writing, but the rate given for the U.S. dollar (1.66) fluctuates, so please be sure to check the rate when you buy your passes.

Now, this can seem a little expensive, but let's take a look and see:

Suppose you want to visit the Tower of London (£19.50 per person), Westminster Abbey (£18), the Churchill War Rooms (£15.45), Windsor Castle (£17.75), Hampton Court Palace (£16) and, perhaps, take in River Cruise (£17). Individually, that list adds up to some £103 ($170) per person. But you won't be able to do all that in a single day. Because of the geography, and the time needed on site, you will need to allow three days to cover that short list. A three-day adult pass costs £77 ($128), so the saving would be quite significant (£30 or $50, per person) add in a couple more attractions in central London and you'll be making out like a bandit.

You can also purchase the London Pass with a travel option included; and that's really nice because for just an additional £9 per day for the adult pass, and £4 per day for a child's pass, you get unlimited travel on the Tube, trains and buses. If you have decided not to go with the Oyster Card, this would be a good option for you, but you'll need to make the purchase prior to your arrival in London.

Buy your London Passes at londonpass.com

The London Pass offers one more goodie: it comes with a guidebook and a fold-out map of London's Tube system map; quite handy, really.

The Attractions:

I have listed below those attractions I think are must-visits. I have visited each and every one of them; some more than once; some many times. If you can fit them all into a single trip, I admire you. If you have time for only a few of them, I suggest you follow my lead and try to include those I have poster with 4 or more Stars (*). Some, I haven't rated at all, but that doesn't mean they are not worth visiting; it just means I consider them to be less important that those I have rated, but well worth a visit nonetheless.

The London Eye has become London's premier tourist attraction, and it really is not to be missed. Standing some 430 feet high, with 32 observation capsules, the Eye provides visitors with stunning views over the river and city, and for more than 20 miles in any direction. More than 3.5 million visitors ride the great wheel each year, making it the most popular attraction in the city, if not the entire UK.

Photo Courtesy of Creative Commons and McKay Savage

The 32 egg-shaped passenger capsules – one for each of the 32 London Boroughs - are sealed and air-conditioned. Seating is provided for up to 25 people, but you are free to walk around inside the capsule. The wheel rotates very slowly – it is not a Ferris wheel – and takes about 30 minutes to complete one revolution. The wheel does not stop to take on passengers; the speed of rotation is slow enough for passengers to board and exit while the capsules are at ground level. The wheel stops only to accommodate handicapped or elderly passengers.

A Capsule at the top of the London Eye - Photo Courtesy of Creative Commons and Gabriel Villena

The London Eye is a must, especially if you're visiting London for the first time.

So, how much does it cost to ride London's premier attraction? Well, it's not cheap. For one adult, or child over four years of age, the fare is £29.50 – almost $50 (if you buy tickets in advance online you'll pay £25.55 – you save 10%); you can purchase a ticket for a family of four for £118.00 – almost $200 (£94.40 if you buy in advance online).

This attraction DOES NOT take the London Pass

Tickets can be booked online at londoneye.com, and I recommend you do just that; you might even find there are extra savings available if you check in early enough. If you decide to wait and pay at the Eye, you can but you may have to wait a short while before boarding. Don't be put off by what appear to be long lines; things move quite quickly. Oh, and don't forget your camera. Just take a look at the image below. It shows just what photo opportunities are available from the top of the Eye.

Opening Hours:

The attraction is open from 10am until 8:30pm September 1 through the end of March, and from 10am until 9:30pm May through October. The exceptions being Christmas even when the Eye closes at 5pm, New Year's Eve when it closes at 3pm; the Eye is closed on Christmas Day.

View from the top of the London Eye of the Houses of Parliament - Photo Courtesy of Creative Commons and Lokai Profil

Important Note:

I've listed the next three attractions together. They are all within a few hundred yards of one another, so it makes sense to put them together here; you can, in fact, visit all three in a single day.

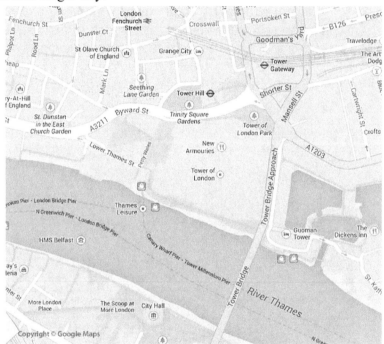

Tower Hill, London Bridge and HMS Belfast –
Courtesy of Google Maps

The Tower of London*****

I have visited the Tower of London a number of times over the years. It is a vast complex with a long and varied history, and each time I visit, there's always something new going on. Despite the Tower of London's grim reputation as a place of torture and death, within these walls you will also discover its history as a royal palace, prison, armory and a great fortress.

The Tower of London as seen from the river Thames –
Photo Courtesy of Creative Commons and Bob Cowan

You'll also be able to view the priceless Crown Jewels, tour the Tower with one of the iconic Beefeaters and hear their bloody tales; you can stand on the spot where Queens Anne Boleyn, Catherine Howard and Lady Jane Grey lost their heads, and learn the legend of the Tower's ravens.

Her Majesty's Royal Palace and Fortress, more commonly known as the Tower of London, is an historic castle located on the north bank of the River Thames in central London on Tower Hill. It has its beginnings in 1066 when, shortly after the Norman Conquest; the White Tower, which gives the entire castle its name, was built by William the Conqueror in 1078. From then on, the Tower has played a prominent role in English history. It has served as an armory, a treasury, a menagerie (it was London's first zoo), the home of the Royal Mint, a public records office, and the home of the Crown.

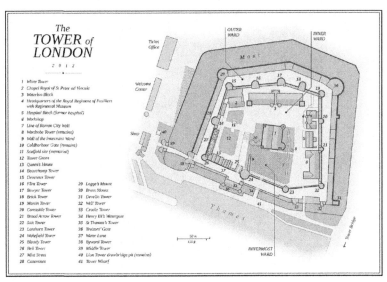

Image Courtesy of Creative Commons

In the late 15th century the castle was the prison of the Princes in the Tower: Edward V of England and Richard of Shrewsbury, Duke of York. The two brothers were the only sons of Edward IV of England and Elizabeth Woodville still alive at the time of their father's death. The boys were 12 and 9 years old when they were lodged in the Tower by the man appointed to look after them, their uncle, the Lord Protector: Richard, Duke of Gloucester. This was supposed to be in preparation for Edward's coronation as king. However, Richard took the throne for himself and the boys disappeared. It is thought by many that Richard had them both murdered, but that has never been proved, nor is likely to be.

Under the Tudors, the Tower became used less as a royal residence and more as a prison to house the many members of the nobility who had fallen into disgrace, such as Elizabeth I before she became queen. This use has led to the phrase "sent to the Tower". Despite its enduring reputation as a place of torture and death, only seven people were executed within the Tower. Almost all executions were public affairs held on the notorious Tower Hill to the north of the castle; there were some 112 executions there over a period of 400 years.

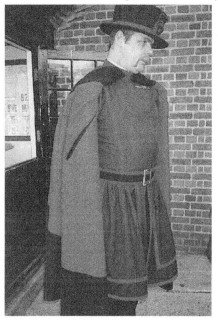

Beefeater (Yeoman of the Guard) at the Tower of London – Photo Courtesy of Creative Commons and Colin Smith

During the First and Second World Wars, the Tower was again used as a prison, and was the place of execution of 12 men for espionage. Under the ceremonial charge of the Constable of the Tower, it is cared for by the charity Historic Royal Palaces and is protected as a World Heritage Site.

The Jewel House

My first visit to the Jewel House was in 1968; That Jewel House was an underground vault built in the west wing of the Waterloo Barracks in 1967. The entrance was in the west front of the barracks, with the basement chamber being entered through the ground floor chamber, down 49 steps, past untreated concrete walls, and through a massive strong-room door. The vault was said to be nuclear bomb proof, and to contain electronic beams and steel shutters for security. The jewels were displayed in a series of glass cases arranged in a circle, around which visitors walked/shuffled clockwise, under the supervision of the wardens.

The Jewel House was originally designed to host about a million visitors each year. By 1980, however, it was catering to more than two million visitors per year.

The Waterloo Barracks – Photo Courtesy of Creative Commons and Cherry X

The new Jewel House, the one you'll visit, was built is 1994; it is also housed in the Waterloo Barracks, but at ground level. The display area is three times the size of the old Jewel House, and can cope with 2,500 visitors an hour. This is achieved by the use of a moving pavement.

The Chapel Royal of St. Peter ad Vincula ("St. Peter in chains"), located within the Tower's inner ward, is the parish church of the Tower of London and dates from 1520.

The Chapel Royal of St. Peter ad Vincula – Photo Courtesy of Creative Commons

The Chapel is the final resting place of some of the Tower of London's most famous prisoners, including three queens: Anne Boleyn and Catherine Howard, the second and fifth wives of Henry VIII, respectively, and Lady Jane Grey, who reigned for nine days in 1553.

George Boleyn, brother of Anne, was also buried in the Chapel here after his execution in 1536, as were Edmund Dudley, Guildford Dudley (husband to Lady Jane Grey), Sir Thomas More (one-time chancellor of England under Henry VIII) and Bishop John Fisher, who also incurred the wrath of Henry VIII; both were executed, and later canonized as martyrs by the Roman Catholic Church. In addition, Henry VIII's minister, Thomas Cromwell, executed in 1540, was buried in the Chapel. Who would want to work for good King Henry?

The Chapel can be visited during a tour within the Tower of London.

Adults - £19.50 ($32) per ticket

Children 5 to 15 - £9.75 ($16) per ticket

Children under 5 free.

This attraction takes the London Pass

The Tower and Grounds are open Sundays and Mondays from 10am until 4:30pm, and Tuesday through Saturday from 9am until 4:30pm.

Tower Bridge****:

If you're visiting the Tower of London, it makes sense to walk down to the Embankment and at least view the great bridge, close-up. Tower Bridge, built during the years 1886 to1894, is a combined bascule (the word "bascule" is French for see-saw, and refers to the lower lifting section of the bridge) and suspension bridge in London which crosses the River Thames. It is close to the Tower of London, from which it takes its name, and has become an iconic symbol of London.

Tower Bridge as Seen from the Embankment at the Tower of London – Photo Courtesy of Creative Commons and Matt Buck

The bridge consists of two towers tied together at the upper level by means of two horizontal walkways, designed to withstand the horizontal forces exerted by the suspended sections of the bridge on the landward sides of the towers. The vertical component of the forces in the suspended sections and the vertical reactions of the two walkways are carried by the two robust towers. The bascule pivots and operating machinery are housed in the base of each tower.

One of the Great Steam Engines in Tower Bridge – Photo Courtesy of Creative Commons

In days gone by, Tower Bridge was powered by steam engines. Today it is powered by electric motors and is raised about 1,000 times a year to allow tall ships, cruise ships, naval vessels, etc., to pass through into the Pool of London

The Tower Bridge Exhibition

Tower Bridge is, I think, THE iconic view in London. The views over the city and River Thames you can enjoy from its upper-level walkways are stunning, to say the least. Allow at least an hour and a half if you want to do the full Tower Bridge experience.

Tickets and Admissions:

Adults: £8

Children 5 to 15: £3.40

You can use your London Pass for this attraction

How to Get There:

By Tube:

The nearest Tube Station is London Bridge – go via either Northern or Jubilee Lines

By Bus:

Routes: RV1, 17, 21, 35, 40, 43, 47, 133, 141, 149, 343, 381, 521 (or any **bus** to London Bridge) all serve London Bridge and HMS Belfast.

Opening Hours

The Bridge Exhibition is Open Daily

April - September: 10am - 6pm (last admission 5.30pm)

October - March: 9.30am - 5.30pm (last admission 5pm)

Closed 24 and 25 December. Open from 12pm midday on 1 January.

Address:

Tower Bridge Exhibition

Tower Bridge

London, SE1 2UP

Where to Eat:

Try the Draft House at the Tower of London; they do a great burger there:

Inside the Draft House – Photo Courtesy of Creative Commons

HMS Belfast is a World War ii era warship of the British Royal navy, now a museum. You can see HMS Belfast from the Embankment at the Tower of London; it's moored just across the river. Belfast is a proud ship with a long and heroic history. Today, the mighty ship is in retirement and is operated by the Imperial War Museum.

HMS Belfast today, moored close to Tower Bridge in London – Photo Courtesy of Alves Gaspar and Creative Commons

Originally a Royal Navy light cruiser, HMS Belfast was launched on St Patrick's Day, 17 March 1938. Commissioned in early August 1939 shortly before the outbreak of the Second World War, Belfast was initially part of the British naval blockade against Germany.

HMS Belfast bombarding the German Positions at the Normandy landings – Photo Courtesy of Creative Commons

In November 1939 Belfast struck a German mine and spent more than two years undergoing extensive repairs. Returning to action in November 1942 with improved firepower, radar equipment and armor, Belfast was the largest and arguably most powerful cruiser in the Royal Navy at the time.

Belfast saw action escorting Arctic convoys to the Soviet Union during 1943, and in December 1943 played an important role in the Battle of North Cape, assisting in the destruction of the German warship Scharnhorst.

In June 1944 Belfast took part in Operation Overlord supporting the Normandy landings. In June 1945 she was redeployed to the Far East to join the British Pacific Fleet, arriving shortly before the end of the Second World War.

The Belfast Coming alongside the USS Bataan in May 1952 – Photo Courtesy of Creative Commons

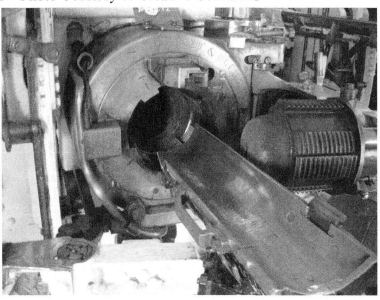

The Breech of one of Belfast's 6-inch guns – Photo Courtesy of Creative Commons

Belfast saw further combat action in 1950–52 during the Korean War and underwent an extensive modernization between 1956 and 1959. A number of further overseas commissions followed before Belfast entered the reserve in 1963.

In 1967, efforts were initiated to avert Belfast's expected scrapping and preserve her as a museum ship. A joint committee of the Imperial War Museum, the National Maritime Museum and the Ministry of Defense was established, and reported in June 1968 that preservation was practical. In 1971 the government decided against preservation, prompting the formation of the private HMS Belfast Trust to campaign for her preservation. The efforts of the Trust were successful, and the government transferred the ship to the Trust in July 1971.

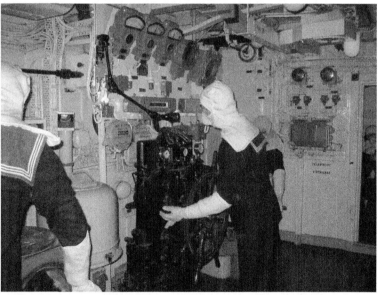

One of the many exhibits within HMS Belfast – Photo Courtesy of Creative Commons

Brought to London, she was moored on the River Thames near Tower Bridge in the Pool of London and opened to the public in October 1971. Belfast became a branch of the Imperial War Museum in 1978.

A popular tourist attraction, Belfast hosts some 250,000 visitors per year. Allow 2 hours for your visit.

Visitor Information

How to Get There:

By Tube:

The nearest Tube Station is London Bridge – go via either Northern or Jubilee Lines

By Bus:

Routes: RV1, 17, 21, 35, 40, 43, 47, 133, 141, 149, 343, 381, 521 (or any **bus** to London Bridge) all serve London Bridge and HMS Belfast.

Opening Hours:

1 March to 31 October: 10am–6pm. Last admission 5pm.

November to February: 10am-5pm. Last admission 4pm.

Closed 24, 25, and 26 December.

Tickets:

Adults: £15.50

Children under 16: Free but must be accompanied by an adult.

You can use your London Pass at this attraction.

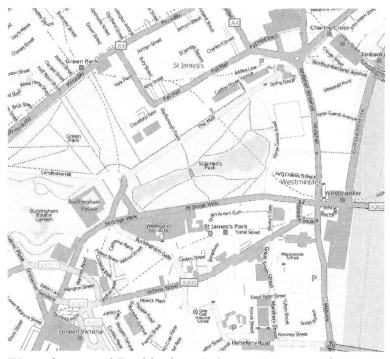

Westminster and Buckingham Palace – Courtesy of Google Maps

Buckingham Palace is Queen Elizabeth II's official residence in London, and has been that of all of Britain's sovereigns since 1837. Before that, the official residence was St. James's Palace, now the home of Princess Royal and Princess Alexandra, the Honorable Lady Ogilvy.

Buckingham Palace once was the home of the Dukes of Buckingham. It was purchased by King George III in 1761 for his wife Queen Charlotte.

The State Rooms at Buckingham Palace have been opened to the public during August and September each year since 1993. If you can spare the time (you'll need to allow two to three hours) and the cost of admission (£75.00 or $125 per person), you really should consider visiting this most amazing palace.

2014 Dates: August 2nd through September 28, 2014: Open daily 9:30am to 7pm

Buckingham Palace operates on a timed-ticket system; admission is at 5 minute intervals throughout the day. Tickets are valid only on the date and at the entrance time specified on the ticket. Be on time for your visit; if you're late, you will not be admitted.

If you are visiting at any other time of year, you'll want to see the Changing of the Guard. It happens on most days of the month, but you'll need to check the actual dates before you go at changing-the-guard.com/dates-times.html. The ceremony begins at 11am with the arrival of Guards and bands, and last for about 45 minutes. This is a popular attraction, so be sure to arrive early to get a good spot.

How to Get There:

By Tube

The nearest Tube stations to Buckingham Palace are Victoria, Green Park, and Hyde Park Corner.

By Bus:

Buses numbered 11, 211, 239, C1, and C10 stop on Buckingham Palace Road.

The Queen's Gallery:

The Queen's Gallery at Buckingham Palace is a museum, of sorts, dedicated presenting exhibitions of items of the Royal Collection, a vast collection of art and treasures "held in trust by The Queen for the Nation." The Gallery was renovated and expanded and reopened by The Queen on 21 May 2002.

The Entrance to the Queen's Gallery – Photo Courtesy of Phillip Perry and Creative Commons

The expansion cost more than £20 million and was funded entirely by the Royal Collection Trust. The exhibitions are ever-changing, but you can expect to see works of art by the great masters, such as Highlights: Expect to see artworks by Peter Paul Rubens, Thomas Gainsborough, Rembrandt, and Canaletto, to name but a few.

The Queen's Gallery is open daily to the public. For what is on, check royalcollection.org.uk.

Opening Hours at the Queen's Gallery:

Open daily, 10am-5:30pm; A typical visit lasts between 1 and 1 hour 30 minutes. The Last admission is at 4:30pm.

The Queen's Gallery is closed:

17 March - 10 April 2014

18 April 2014

13-30 October 2014

25-26 December 2014

Admission to the Queen's Gallery:

Adult £9.50

Over 60/Student (with valid ID) £8.75

Under 17 £4.80

Under 5 Free

Family (2 adults, 3 under 17s) £24.00

A booking fee of £1.25 per ticket applies

You **cannot** use your London Pass for the Queen's Gallery

You can book your tickets online at rcetickets.com.

Note: the exchange rate at the time of writing was $1.66 to £1

The Royal Mews

The Royal Mews at Buckingham Palace is a very busy place; it is responsible getting the queen and members of the Royal Family where they need to go, ostensibly by road – car and horse-drawn carriage.

The Golden Coach at the Royal Mews - – Photo Courtesy of David Crochet and Creative Commons

The Royal Mews has a permanent display of State vehicles, including the Gold State Coach used for Coronations, and a variety of other carriages used for Royal and State occasions: State Visits, weddings, and the State Opening of Parliament. All the Queen's horses, not to mention some of the Queen's men, are stabled at the Royal Mews. If you're visiting Buckingham Palace, it makes good sense to visit the Royal Mews too. Allow at least an hour. You will be allowed to take photos, so take your camera along with you.

Opening Times at the Royal Mews:

3 February - 31 March; Monday to Saturday 10am to 4pm

April 1st – October 31; Monday to Saturday 10am to 5pm

1-30 November Monday to Saturday 10am to 4pm

Admission to the Royal Mews

Adult £8.75

Over 60/Student (with valid ID) £8.00

Under 17 £5.40

Under 5 Free

Family (2 adults, 3 under 17s) £22.90

Note: the exchange rate at the time of writing was $1.66 to £1

You can use your London Pass for the Royal Mews.

You can book your tickets online at rcetickets.com.

Buying Tickets on the day at the Palace

The Ticket Office is at the Visitor Entrance located in Buckingham Palace, on Buckingham Palace Road.

Westminster Abbey*****:

If you've never visited one of England's great churches or cathedrals, Westminster Abbey is a great place to start. Not just a great place to start, but a must visit. I have lost count of the number of times I have visited this amazing, emotionally moving church, but I know I was very young when my mother first took me inside. I remember, even then, that I was filled with awe and amazement, not by its incredible beauty (I was too young to appreciate that), but more with the overpowering feeling of its great space.

Photo Courtesy of Christine Matthews and Creative Commons

Westminster Abbey was founded more than 1,000 years ago by King Edgar in the year 960; back then it was just a very small Benedictine monastery. Today, almost nothing is left of the original building. Sometime during the early 1040s, King Edward the Confessor enlarged the monastery and built a large stone church in honor of St Peter the Apostle. This church, now known as the "west minster" was consecrated on 28 December 1065. King Edward died a few days later and is entombed in front of the High Altar.

King Edward's Abbey survived for two centuries until the middle of the 13th century when King Henry III decided to rebuild it in the new Gothic style of architecture. All that remains of Edward the Confessor's monastery are the round arches and massive supporting columns of the undercroft and the Pyx Chamber in the cloisters. Today, the undercroft houses the Abbey Museum but was originally part of the domestic quarters of the monks.

The Rude Screen – Photo Courtesy of Herri Lawford and and Creative Commons

The 13th century – the 1200s - was the great age for cathedral building: in England, the great cathedrals at Canterbury, Winchester and Salisbury, and in France

Amiens, Evreux and Chartres, were all built during the 13th century. This church was consecrated on 13 October 1269 and is not only a great monastery and place of worship, it is also a place for the coronation and burial of kings, queens and all sorts of famous folk from British history from the past 1,000 years. King Henry III? Well, he died in 1272 and is buried… in Westminster Abbey; where else?

Photo Courtesy of Harland Quarrington and Creative Commons

These days when I visit the great abbey, it's the history that overwhelms me: most of England's Kings and Queens, with a few notable exceptions, were buried here; King John is buried in Worcester Cathedral (his choice), Edward IV, Henry VIII and Charles II are buried in St George's Chapel in Windsor Castle. It truly makes the hair on the back of my neck stand on end when I stand and look at the tombs of Elizabeth 1, Mary, Queen of Scotts, Henry V and his queen, Catherine, and Henry VII the first of the Tudors.

The Incredible Fan Vaulting in Westminster Abbey - Photo Courtesy of Jessica Neal and Creative Commons

Then there are the tombs and memorials of England's great dukes, earls, poets, and a thousand-and one other famous figures throughout Britain's long and colorful history. Then, of course, there is the great church itself: its architecture, the stained glass windows, the vaulted ceilings, and on and on.

The Henry VII Chapel and Stained Glass Window - Photo Courtesy of Herri Lawford and Creative Commons

What to See:

Be sure to visit the tombs of the kings and queens, the Coronation Chair near the Shrine of St. Edward the Confessor, the Coronation robes in the Abbey Museum; Poet's Corner in the South Transept features the tombs and memorials for many of Britain's great and famous writers, including Geoffrey Chaucer, John Dryden, Charles Dickens, Rudyard Kipling, Thomas Hardy, D H Lawrence, John Masefield, and Alfred Lord Tennyson. Try to find time for the Northumberland Chapel where the Seymours and the Percys are entombed. And don't be afraid to ask questions: the Abbey staff are extremely knowledgeable and always willing to help.

How to Get There

Nearest Tube Stations:

Westminster

St. James's Park

By Bus:

Bus Routes: 11, 148, 211, 24, N11, N136, N2, N44 all serve Westminster Abbey

Opening Times:

Monday to Saturday: 9.30am - 4.30pm

Monday, Tuesday, Thursday, Friday: 9.30am-4.30pm (last admission 3.30pm)

Wednesday: 9.30am-7.00pm (last admission 6.00pm)

Saturday: 9.30am-2.30pm (last admission 1.30pm)

On Sundays the Abbey is open for worship only.

Check official website for current opening times.

Admission:

Adults £18.00

Concessions £15.00 (Over 18 students (on production of a valid student card) and 60+)

Children (11 - 18 years) £8; Child under 11 free accompanied by an adult

Family £36.00 (2 adults and 1 child) £44.00 (2 adults and 2 children)

Entry for all the above includes a free audio-guide each

Your London Pass is good for admission to Westminster Abbey

Tours of the Abbey:

Verger-led tours are available for a small additional charge; in English only; the last about an hour and a half and well worth the donation..

Audio tours are also available and take about an hour; they are available in English, German, French, Spanish, Italian, Russian, Mandarin Chinese, and Japanese. You can get them at the Abbey's Information Desk near the North Door.

Photography:

Photography, filming and audio recording of any kind are not allowed in any part of the Abbey at any time. You can, however, take pictures in the Cloisters and College Garden.

Cell/Mobile Phones, Tablets, Etc.:

You can use your cell phone only in the Cloisters and College Garden. Please turn your devices off while you are in the Abbey church.

The Museums and Harrods – Courtesy of Google
Maps

The British Museum*****:

Many years ago, maybe 20 years ago, I was on
assignment in London for a major travel magazine and was
lucky enough to be allowed free, before hours access, with
a camera, to London's premier museums. I was allowed
into six of London's great museums, including this one, the
Natural History Museum, and the Victoria and Albert
Museum.

You have no idea what it was like to have the British
Museum, and the others, all to myself for almost three
hours at a time. The museum staff provided me with a
knowledgeable guide and I was left pretty much to myself
to do what I needed to do. I saw and photographed most
what there was to see at the time. There have been some
changes since then, but the grand old lady of the London
Museum circuit remains much the same as it was all those
years ago. I photographed all of the great galleries and
many of the exhibits therein. Some of those photographs
are reproduced here; some of the photographs are from
other sources:

70

Photographs;

The British Museum – Photo Courtesy of Creative Commons.

Sculpture of Ramesses II Courtesy of Nic McPhee and Creative Commons

71

Photo Copyright © Blair Howard

The Rosetta Stone - Photo Copyright © Blair Howard

The Rosetta Stone in Room 4 of the Ancient Egyptian Gallery is a must see; it is only because of the discovery of this stone that we were able to decipher the hieroglyphics, and, thus able to learn all we know today about ancient Egypt.

Ancient Egyptian Mummies - Photo Copyright © Blair Howard

The Elgin Marbles - Photo Copyright © Blair Howard

The British Museum is the world's largest museum of the humanities, history, art, art and culture. Its treasures include artifacts, statues from ancient Egypt (including a great many mummies), the ancient Rome, Greece, Britain (including artifacts from the Sutton Hoo Anglo-Saxon ship burial) and, of course, you can see the Elgin Marbles (above) from the Parthenon in Greece. And the good news, like all of the UK's national museums,

Not to Be Missed Highlights:

It's not possible to see everything in a single day, but there are some you really should not miss:

The Snettisham Hoard: a collection of 2,000 year old gold jewelry.

The Ancient Egyptian Galleries: Room 4 (Sculpture) and rooms 61 through 66.

Ancient Greece: Rooms 11 through 23

Ancient Rome: Rooms 70 through 85.

The Galleries of the Americas, including Aztec, Mayan, Arctic and Native American exhibitions

The Middle East, including the Assyrians, Babylonians, Hittites, and Sumerians: rooms 6 through 10

The Holy Land: Israelites, Phoenicians, Canaanites and ancient Islamic societies. Room 88.

Museum facilities:

There are four shops where you can buy souvenirs, post cards and collectibles, and there are three restaurants and a family picnic area.

Opening Hours and Admissions

Opening Hours: 10a.m. to 5:30 p.m. every day except Good Friday, January 1 and December 24-26. Late openings to 8:30 p.m. every Thursday and Friday

Admission: Free, though tickets may have to be purchased for some special exhibitions

How to Get There:

Tube Stations: Tottenham Court Road on the Northern Line and Central Lines; and Holborn on the Piccadilly or Central Lines are closest.

Bus services: Routes 1, 7, 8, 19, 25, 38, 55, 98 and 242 all serve the museum via New Oxford Street

This is the second of London's museums I was lucky enough to be allowed free access to. London's Natural History Museum and was able to photograph almost all of the great galleries and many of the exhibits therein. Some of those photographs are reproduced here; some of the photographs are from other sources.

The natural History Museum is truly a stunning place. Nowhere else can view such an amazing display of exhibits and artifacts from the natural sciences as you can here.

The Natural History Museum in London – Photo Courtesy of Creative Commons

The museum is one of the most popular attractions in London and thus is always very busy; expect long lines, especially at weekend, when I do not recommend that you visit. The best time, I think, is early on a weekday morning.

The Natural History Museum is home to more than 70 million artifacts in five main collections: botany, entomology, mineralogy, paleontology and zoology.

The museum is a world-renowned center of research specializing in taxonomy, identification and conservation.

Many of the collections have great historical as well as scientific value, such as specimens collected by Charles Darwin.

The Iconic view of the main gallery of the Natural History Museum in London – Photo Courtesy of Creative Commons

The Whale Room – Photo Courtesy of Denis Bourez and Creative Commons.

The Natural History Museum is world famous for its dinosaur skeletons. You cannot think of the Natural History Museum in London without thinking... dinosaur. Dinosaurs are what the museum is most famous for, but there a whole lot more to it than that.

This is vast a museum, one of three large museums on Exhibition Road in South Kensington, the others being the Science Museum and the Victoria and Albert Museum; the Natural History Museum's main frontage is, however, on Cromwell Road.

But, as I have already mentioned, the museum is particularly famous for its exhibition of dinosaur skeletons, as you see the large Diplodocus which dominates the central hall. The Natural History Museum Library contains an extensive collection of books, journals, manuscripts, and artwork. Here are some photos of interest:

Megatherium Skeleton Photo Courtesy of Drow-Male and Creative Commons

Triceratops - Photo Copyright © Blair Howard

Stegosaurus - Photo Copyright © Blair Howard

Meteors in the natural History Museum - Photo Copyright © Blair Howard

How to Get There

Nearest Tube Station:

South Kensington

Opening Hours:

Seven days a week: 10am - 5.50pm

The Museum is open every day except 24-26 December.

Last admission is at 5.30pm.

Tickets:

Admission is free to the permanent displays but tickets are needed for temporary exhibitions.

I have to admit, that the Victoria and Albert Museum is not one of my favorite places to visit. It's huge, and I even find it a little depressing. Having said that, there are some really interesting collections housed within.

The V&A – Victoria and Albert Museum - Photo Copyright © Blair Howard

The Victoria and Albert Museum, known by Londoners as the V&A, is the world's largest museum of decorative arts and design, housing a permanent collection of more than 4.5 million artifacts ranging from the antiquities to modern times, including fashion, furniture, ceramics, photography, sculpture, jewelry, clothing, textiles, decorative objects, even tombs.

This is another of London's great museums that will take more time to visit than you can probably spare. So, with that in mind, there are some items you should try not to miss:

Pietro Torrigiani's colored terracotta bust of Henry VII, dated 1509–11

Henry VII – Photo Courtesy of Creative Commons

Henry VIII's writing desk, dated 1525, made from walnut and oak, lined with leather and painted and gilded with the king's coat of arms

A spinet dated 1570–1580, made for Elizabeth I

The Great Bed of Ware, dated 1590–1600, a large, elaborately carved four-poster bed with marquetry headboard. The bed was made famous by William Shakespeare; he featured it in Twelfth Night

The Great Bed of Ware – Photo Courtesy of Creative Commons

Bernini's bust of Thomas Barker, dated c1638

17th-century tapestries from the Sheldon and Mortlake workshops

The wood relief of The Stoning of St Stephen, dated c1670, by Grinling Gibbons

The Macclesfield Wine Set, dated 1719–1720, made by Anthony Nelme, the only complete set known to survive.

The life-size sculpture of George Frederick Handel, dated 1738, by Louis-François Roubiliac

Numerous items of furniture by Thomas Chippendale and Robert Adam

Henry VIII's writing desk. Many of his love letters to Anne Bolyn were written at this desk.

James III's wedding suit

King James III Wedding Suite – Photo Courtesy of Creative Commons

Drawings by Inigo Jones: The pen and ink architectural pictures are kept in a set of drawers that you can open to get close to the works of one of the 17th century's most famous draftsmen and designers.

The museum also owns many stunning pieces by renowned jewelers Cartier, Jean Schlumberger, Peter Carl Fabergé and Lalique. Other items in the collection include diamond dress ornaments made for Catherine the Great, bracelet clasps once belonging to Marie Antoinette, and the Beauharnais emerald necklace presented by Napoleon to his adopted daughter Hortense de Beauharnais in 1806.

Golf Alter and Processional Crosses – Photo Courtesy of Creative Commons

How to Get There:

Nearest Tube Station

London Underground stop:South Kensington on the District, Circle and Piccadilly lines.

By Bus:

Buses C1, 14, 74 and 414 stop outside the Cromwell Road entrance.

Opening Hours and Admissions

Admission is free

Museum opening hours

10am to 5.45pm daily

10am to 10pm on Fridays

Last admissions: 10 minutes before time stated

Closed 24, 25 and 26 December

The tunnel entrance to the V&A is open from 10am to 5:40pm Saturday to Thursday and 10am to 8pm on Fridays, but may be closed on occasion on the advice of London Underground.

Tate Britain, formerly known as the Tate Gallery, houses a vast collection of British art dating from around 1500 to today. There are actually four 'Tates': two in London - Tate Britain and Tate Modern. Then there are Tate Liverpool and Tate St Ives, which is in the town of that name in Cornwall. You can view the entire Tate Collection online, should you wish to do so. The individual galleries within are arranged in chronological order.

Tate Britain – Photo Courtesy of Creative Commons

I have visited Tate Britain a few times over the past 30 years, or so, but I have to tell you, it's not one of my favorites. I think you have to have a real interest in art and artists to get the full benefit of what is undoubtable one of the world's finest collections of historic and contemporary art.

Tate Britain houses collections of paintings by the old masters - Gainsborough, Peter Paul Rubens, J.M.W. Turner, Joshua Reynolds, Anthony van Dyck, John Constable, and many, many more. It takes a while to get through all the galleries so, if you love art, and then Tate Britain is for you, but you'll need to allow at least a half a day, and that really will be a bit of flying visit.

London_from_Greenwich by J.W.M. Turner – Image Courtesy of Creative Commons

Opening Hours and Admissions:

Open daily: 10am - 5.50pm

Exhibitions open: 10am - 5.40pm

Closed 24, 25, 26 December (open as normal on 1 January).

Entrance to the Museum is free, but you'll be expected to make a £4 donation. (your London Pass will work instead)

How to Get There:

Nearest Tube Station:

Pimlico

By Bus:

Route 87 stops on Millbank

Routes 88 and C10 stop on John Islip Street

Routes 2, 36, 185, 436 stop on Vauxhall Bridge Road

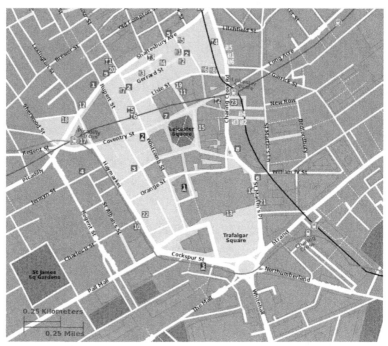

Trafalgar Square – Courtesy of Creative Commons

Trafalgar Square****:

No visit to London would be complete without a visit to Trafalgar Square. Built around a section of central London that once was known as Charing Cross, the square is part of the City of Westminster. Trafalgar Square is dominated by Nelson's Column, which stands at its center and is guarded by four bronze lions sculpted by Sir Edwin Landseer. The column is topped by a statue of Horatio Nelson, the vice admiral who commanded the British Fleet at Trafalgar.

Trafalgar Square – Photo Courtesy of Creative Commons

The fountains you see in the square are fairly new. Designed by Sir Edwin Lutyens, they were installed in the 1930s at a cost of almost £50,000.

The pump system was replaced in 2009; the new pump is capable of sending an 80-foot jet of water into the air. A new LED lighting system was also installed.

The square is also used for political demonstrations and community gatherings, such as the celebration of New Year's Eve.

On the north side of the square is the National Gallery and to its east St Martin-in-the-Fields Church. To the south is Whitehall, to the east the Strand and South Africa House; to the north is Charing Cross Road, and Canada House is on the west side of the square.

Trafalgar Square on New Years Eve – Photo Courtesy of Elliott Brown and Creative Commons

How to Get There:

Nearest Tube Stations:

Trafalgar Square Tube Station is 3 minutes from Trafalgar Square

Leicester Square Tube Station is 5 minutes from Trafalgar Square Embankment Underground Station

Villiers Street Tube Station is 5 minutes from Trafalgar Square

You can walk to the square from any of the above stations.

By Bus:

Bus Routes 12, 13, 139, 15, 159, 23, 3, 453, 6, 88, N109, N113, N13, N136, N3 all serve Trafalgar Square.

If you've never visited London before, you'll not want to miss the Houses of Parliament. The Palace of Westminster, the one-time primary London residence of the Kings of England, is now the home of Britain's House of Commons and House of Lords, the two houses of the Parliament of the United Kingdom.

The Palace of Westminster at Sunset – Photo Courtesy of Creative Commons

The palace of Westminster, commonly known as the Houses of Parliament, is located on the banks of the River Thames in the City of Westminster, in central London. Its name, is derived from the neighboring Westminster Abbey. The Old Palace, a medieval building, was destroyed by fire in 1834, and it is its replacement, the New Palace, that you see today. For ceremonial purposes, the palace retains its original style and status as a royal residence.

Above: The Houses of Parliament St. Stephens Hall (Interior) London; shows statues of many of Britain's most famous prime minister and members of parliament. Photo Courtesy of Creative Commons.

The first royal palace was built on the site in the eleventh century and was home to England's royalty until most of it was destroyed by fire in 1512. After that, it served as the home of Parliament, which had been meeting there since the thirteenth century. The Palace is also the seat of the Royal Courts of Justice. In 1834, an even greater fire ravaged the rebuilt Houses of Parliament, and the only structures of significance to survive were Westminster Hall, the Cloisters of St Stephen's, the Chapel of St Mary Undercroft and the Jewel Tower.

Major conservation work has been underway almost constantly ever since the reconstruction, mostly to combat the ravages air pollution. The Palaces contains some 1,200 rooms, more than two miles of passages and corridors, and almost 100 staircases.

Guided Tours of the Palace:

During the summer, August through September, Monday through Saturday, when parliament is not in session, visitors can buy tickets to tour both houses of Parliament. The tours last an hour and fifteen minutes; they start every 15 minutes and include groups of about 20. Tours are led qualified guides.

Best time to tour is in the morning; it get very busy in the afternoons. Saturday tours are available throughout the year. Tours include the chambers of both the House of Commons and the House of Lords, the Queen's Robing Room, the Royal Gallery, the Central Lobby and St Stephen's Hall.

Ticket Information

Weekday and Saturday tours cost the same: £23.59 (About $39). You can book online at Ticketmaster.co.un, or by phone at 0844 847 1672. The London Pass was not accepted at the time of writing.

Security:

Bags larger than those permitted in aircraft cabins may be refused entry. Parliament does not have a left-luggage office, so ladies please leave your larger bags at the hotel.

Tour Rules and regulations:

You must arrive 20 minutes before start of the tour; photography is not allowed except in Westminster Hall; turn of all mobile/cell phones and mobile devices, tablets, etc.; you will not be allowed to leave the tour once it has started; eating, drinking is not allowed inside the Palace; and, of course, no weapons of any kind are allowed.

How to Get There:

By Tube:

The nearest Tube Station is Westminster. The palace is directly across from the station.

By Bus:

Routes 214, C2 and C11 all serve Westminster

Address:

Palace of Westminster, Westminster, London, SW1A 0AA

I don't suppose there are many people who have not heard of Sherlock Holmes and Doctor Watson, especially with all the TV shows featuring the dynamic duo. Sherlock Holmes, master detective, and his long-suffering sidekick, Dr. Watson supposedly lived in lodgings at 221B Baker Street in London between 1881 and1904. And, yes, the address does exist. The big question is, of course: Did Sherlock Holmes and Doctor Watson ever really live there? Of course not; they are after all fictional characters created by Sir Arthur Conan Doyle. But, had they existed in real life, they certainly could have lived there; the building was indeed a lodging house from 1860 to 1934.

The Entrance to the Sherlock Holmes Museum - Courtesy of Creative Commons.

Today, the four story 221B Baker Street building is a museum dedicated to the life and times of the great detective. The ground floor houses the museum shop with staff in dressed in Victorian costume, while the first floor is set up as Mr. Holmes' study, decorated and furnished just as it would have been in Victorian Times.

Sherlock Holmes' Sitting Room - Courtesy of Creative Commons.

Doctor Watson's bedroom and Mrs. Hudson's room she was their landlady - are on the third floor and have displays of waxwork models of some of the main characters in the Sherlock Holmes stories.

Holmes' Lab – Courtesy of Creative Commons

Victorian Bathroom at the Sherlock Holmes Museum - Courtesy of Creative Commons

The shop sells a wide variety of souvenirs and gifts all related to the Sherlock Holmes theme, including deerstalker hats, curly pipes, post cards, books and so on. The rooms on the second floor include Holmes' bedroom, and his study overlooking Baker Street - you can sit in his armchair by the fireplace and get your photo taken wearing the famous deerstalker hat.

When you have completed your visit to the Sherlock Holmes Museum, you can walk on down the road and visit Madame Tussauds which is on the other side of Baker Street Tube station.

How to Get There:

By Tube:

The nearest Tube station is Baker Street

From the Baker Street station, turn right, go cross the road and turn right. It's a walk of about five minutes.

By Bus:

Routes 13 and 139 run between Baker Street and Trafalgar Square.

Address:

221b Baker Street, London NW1 6XE

Tickets and Admissions:

Adult: £8, Child (Under 16): Under £5

Opening Times:

Open every day of the year (except Christmas Day) from 9.30am - 6pm

Madam Tussauds

I think the first time I visited Madam Tussauds I was not much more than 8 years old and can't really remember a whole lot about it. What I do remember is the feeling that the waxworks were all real people standing very still. You may well feel the same. In fact, I was told at the time that the police man standing close to the entrance was indeed real, but even though I remember watching very carefully, he never did move, not even an eyebrow. Cool!

Madam Tussauds – Photo Courtesy of Creative Commons

Madam Tussauds London is one of several such wax museums around the world. The original museum was founded by wax sculptor Marie Tussaud. Madame Tussauds is a major tourist attraction in London, displaying waxworks of historical and royal figures, film stars, sports stars and infamous murderers. Madame Tussauds is owned and operated by Merlin Entertainments.

Lady Diana at Madam Tussauds – Photo Courtesy of Creative Commons

Address:

Madame Tussauds, Marylebone Road, London NW1 5LR

How to Get There:

By Tube:

The nearest Tube Station is Baker Street

By Bus:

Routes 13, 18, 27, 30, 74, 82, 113, 139, 189, 205, 274 and 453 all serve Madam Tussauds

Johnny Depp – Jack Sparrow at Madam Tussauds – Photo Courtesy of Creative Commons

General Opening Times: Daily, 9.30am - 5.30pm. Last admission: 5.30pm.

Daily, 9am - 6pm. Last admission: 6pm.

The museum offers free Wi-Fi so that you can share your photos from your smartphone. Password details are posted around the museum.

Admission:

Adults aged 16 or over: The online price is £22.50; if you buy on the day at the museum, the price is £30

Children are aged 4 to 15: £19.29 online and £25.80 on the day

Children under 4 go free; All children under 16 must be accompanied by an adult aged 16 or over.

Family tickets are for 1 adult and 3 children or 2 adults and 2 children: £83.69 online and £111.60 on the day.

And there are also several other option if you check online at madametussauds.com/London.

The London Pass is not accepted.

Note: Pushchairs (strollers, buggies) are not allowed in the museum and must be left at the collection point.

This is definitely one for American visitors to London. The Benjamin Franklin House at 36 Craven Street, London is a museum in a terraced Georgian house that was, for 16 years from 757 to 1775, the home of its namesake, Benjamin Franklin. The house was built sometime around 1730 and is, in fact, the only surviving former residence of Benjamin Franklin, one of the Founding Fathers of the United States. The museum opened to the public on 17 January 2006.

The Benjamin Franklin House – Photo Courtesy of Creative Commons

Opening Hours

Historical Experience shows run Wednesday to Sunday at:

12 noon, 1pm, 2pm, 3.15pm and 4.15pm

Architectural tours run on Mondays at:

12 noon, 1pm, 2pm, 3.15pm and 4.15pm

Admission:

Adult; £7 Children under 16 free.

The London Pass is accepted here.

Please arrive at the House 10 minutes before your chosen show or tour time. Historical Experience shows last for 45 minutes, and Architectural tours last for 25 minutes.

Tickets:

The Benjamin Franklin House Box Office is open 10:30am-5pm, everyday except Tuesdays. Visit the Box Office to buy tickets and for further information about the House. On Wednesday to Sunday we run Historical Experience shows, and on Mondays we run architectural tours at the following times.

Address:

36 Craven Street

London

WC2N 5NF

How to Get There:

By Tube;

The Benjamin Franklin House is close to Trafalgar Square. The nearest Tube Station is Charing Cross

By Bus:

Bus Routes: 6, 9, 11, 13, 15, 23, 77a all serve the Benjamin Franklin House.

There's not much I can say about the Churchill Museum and Cabinet War Rooms. I'm not old enough to remember those dark days, but my parents and grandparents all suffered through the World War II. I remember only Churchill in opposition (he was already 65 years old at the start of the war) and his magnificent state funeral. The Churchill Museum is the only one of its kind in the world.

Churchill Museum and Cabinet War Rooms House – Photo Courtesy of Creative Commons

The Churchill Museum is dedicated to his life and times, while the Cabinet War Rooms are supposedly just as they were when Churchill and his government directed the action during World War II from 1939 to 1945. You can see the rooms where Churchill made the historic decisions, where he lived and slept, and the war rooms themselves.

I've visited the museum a couple of times. It never gets old, and it's quite an experience, and it's also one you shouldn't miss, but you'll need to allow at least a couple of hours.

The Map Room inside the Churchill Museum and Cabinet War Rooms House – Photo Courtesy of Creative Commons

As is the HMS Belfast, the Churchill Museum and Cabinet War Rooms are operated by the Imperial War Museum.

How to Get There:

By Tube:

Tube Stations:

Westminster (Jubilee, District and Circle Line)

St James's Park (District and Circle Line)

By Bus:

Routes 3, 11, 12, 24, 53, 87, 88, 109, 148, 159, 184, 211, 453 all serve the Churchill Museum

Opening Hours:

Open Daily: 9.30am – 6pm.

Last admission is 5pm.

Open daily except 24, 25, and 26 December.

Admission:

Adults £17.50

Child (under 16) Free

The London Pass is accepted at this attraction

Harrods****

No visit to London would be entirely complete without at least a flying visit to Harrods. However, if you do decide to visit this mighty department store, it would be best if you allowed the best part of a day; there are more than 30 restaurants and snack bars within, so that alone gives you an idea of how big Harrods is. Harrods, located on Brompton Road in Knightsbridge, in the Royal Borough of Kensington and Chelsea, occupies a five-acre site with more than one million square feet of selling space in some 330 departments making it the largest department store in Europe.

Photo Courtesy of Creative Commons

The store's 330 departments offer a wide range of products and services, including clothing for women, men, children and infants, electronics, jewelry, sporting gear, bridal, pets and pet accessories, toys, food and drink, health and beauty items, packaged gifts, stationery, housewares, home appliances, furniture, and much more.

Inside the Oyster bar at Harrods - Photo Courtesy of Creative Commons

Its 32 restaurants serve just about everything you've ever heard of, from high tea to pub food to haute cuisine. There's also pharmacy; a full-service spa and salon; a barbers shop; Harrods Financial Services; Harrods Bank; Ella Jade Bathroom Planning and Design Service; private events planning and catering; food delivery; a wine steward; "picnic" hampers and gift boxes; cakes and pastries of every shape, size and cost, and so and so on.

The Food Hall at Harrods - Photo Courtesy of Creative Commons

The Egyptian Room - Photo Courtesy of Creative Commons

More than a quarter million shoppers visit the store daily, and there are more than 5,000 employees from over fifty different countries working within its walls.

How to Get There:

Address:

Harrods Ltd, 87-135 Brompton Road, Knightsbridge, London SW1X 7XL

By Tube:

The nearest Tube Station is Knightsbridge

By Bus:

Bus routes C1, 74, 414 and 14 all serve the Brompton Road and Harrods.

Opening Hours:

Store: Monday to Saturday 10am to 8pm / Sunday 11.30am to 6pm

Food Halls: Monday to Saturday 9am to 9pm / Sunday 11:30am to 6pm

Selfridges***:

So, you've done Harrods, you might as well go whole hog and do Selfridges as well. Selfridges, on Oxford Street in London (yes, there are others scattered around the UK) is the second largest department store in Britain, after Harrods.

Selfridges on Oxford Street in London - Photo Courtesy of Creative Commons

The store was founded by Harry Gordon Selfridge. The flagship store on London's Oxford Street is the second largest shop in the UK (after Harrods) and opened 15 March 1909.[2]

Selfridges were then taken over in 1965 by the Sears Group owned by Charles Clore. The company grew under the Sears brand with new stores opening in Manchester and Birmingham. But, as we all know, all was/is not well with Sears, and Selfridges was acquired by Canada's Galen Weston in 2003 for £598 million.

Maybe you watched dramatization of the history of Selfridges as shown in the 2013 television series, "Mr. Selfridge."

How to Get There:

By Tube:

Selfridges is at the top end of Oxford Street near to Marble Arch. The closest Tube station is Bond Street on the Central line. Exit at West One.

By Bus

Bus routes: 10, 390, 73, N73, N98 all serve Oxford Street and Selfridges

Opening Hours:

Monday   9:30 am – 9:00 pm

Tuesday   9:30 am – 9:00 pm

Wednesday   9:30 am – 9:00 pm

Thursday 9:30 am – 9:00 pm

Friday   9:30 am – 9:00 pm

Saturday 9:30 am – 9:00 pm

Sunday   11:30 am – 6:00 pm

Okay, so you're visiting London, but I know that sometime during your visit you're going to need to take a break from the hustle and bustle of the big city, time to just take it easy and relax; we all do. That being said, there are any number of day trips you can enjoy, some of them close to London, such as Hampton Court Palace and Windsor Castle, and some of them just a little farther away, like Stratford upon Avon and Shakespeare Country, the Cotswolds and Stonehenge. And, of course, there are a whole lot more, but these five are the iconic visitor attractions outside of London, and all are within easy reach of the city by car, train, bus or guided tour. So let's begin with Hampton Court Palace:

The Great Gate House - Photo Courtesy of Creative Commons and Steve Cadman

Hampton Court Palace is a royal palace set on the banks of the River Thames in the London Borough of Richmond. Although it is still designated a royal palace, it has not been inhabited by the British Royal Family since the 18th century.

Hampton Court was originally owned by Cardinal Thomas Wolsey, King Henry VIII's most trusted advisor. Wolsey took over the property from the Order of St John of Jerusalem in 1514. Over the seven years that followed, Wolsey spent a huge fortune, some 200,000 gold crowns (about £100,000 back then; about £14 million in today's terms), according to the records, to turn it into the finest palace in England; and King Henry VIII had a real problem with that, and so did his soon-to-be queen, Anne Boleyn.

Wolsey fell from favor (something about a divorce☺) and, in trying to appease his volatile king, he offered him the palace as a gift, which the noble Henry immediately accepted☺. Henry then began work to enlarge and improve the grand palace, and for a while he even called it home.

Wren's South Front - Photo Courtesy of Creative Commons

Then, in 1689, Sir Christopher Wren demolished large sections of Wolsey's Tudor palace and began building a new palace for King William III and Queen Mary II. Today, little remains of Wolsey's great palace: just the first courtyard, the Base Court, the second, inner gatehouse which leads to the Clock Court where Wolsey's great seal is still visible over the entrance arch of the clock tower which contained his private rooms.

Even so, Hampton Court remains one of the most important palaces in Britain, and home to a major part of Queen Elizabeth II's Royal Collection, most of which is associated with Hampton Court and dates the 16th and 17th centuries. It really is worth a visit. There's no experience quite like wandering the great state rooms, courtyards and gardens.

What to See:

The Tudor Kitchens:

Dating from 1529, the great kitchens included some 55 rooms spread over more than 3,000 square feet and staffed by more than 200 people serving 600 meals twice daily to the Royal court – photo courtesy of Creative Commons.

The Ceiling of the Great Hall - Photo Courtesy of Creative Commons

The Great Hall:

Great Hall served at the King's dining hall and is one of the finest examples of Tudor architecture.

The Chapel Royal:

The chapel has been in continuous use for over 450 years.

The Ceiling of the Chapel Royal - Photo Courtesy of
Creative Commons and Jodie Bowie

Hampton Court Palace Gardens:

More than 60 acres of gardens stretch all the way down
to the banks of the River Thames. The flowers, when in
bloom, are stunning.

How to Get There:

Hampton Court Palace is in the County of Surrey on
the banks of the River Thames south west of London.

Hampton Court Gardens - Photo Courtesy of Creative Commons and David Stanley

Address:

Hampton Court Palace, East Molesey, Surrey, KT8 9AU

By Tube:

The nearest tube stations is Richmond; from there you'll take the R68 bus and then change to the 111 bus

By Train:

Trains run direct from London Waterloo station to Hampton Court, a trip of about 35 minutes with five-minute from the station to the palace.

By Bus:

Bus routes 111, 216, 411, 451, 461, R68, 513 all serve the palace.

Opening Times:

Monday - Sunday10am - 4:30pm

Last admission3:30pm

Last entry to the maze3:45pm

The Palace and Gardens are closed 24, 25, 26 December.

Admission:

Adult £17.60 (online £16.50)

Children under 16: £8.80 (online £8.25)

Your London Pass can be used at Hampton Court Palace.

Online Booking:
ticketslive.hrp.org.uk/hrp/b2c/index.cfm/calendar/eventCode/HADM

Telephone booking:

0844 482 7799 / 020 3166 6000

In person:

Tickets can be purchased on site at the Palace ticket office which is just inside the main gates.

Audio guides to the palace, in more than a dozen languages, are included in the ticket price and are avauilable at the Information Center in the Base Court.

Disabled Visitors:

Manual wheelchairs are available for use within the palace and single-person scooters are available for use in the gardens only. Neither can be booked in advance.

Windsor Castle is one of Queen Elizabeth's favorite residences. Situated in the county of Berkshire, the castle was built by William the Conqueror in the 11th century not long after the Norman Conquest of England. Back then it was not what it is today: more a wooden fort than stone fortress. William, however, did not use it as a residence. In fact, it was not until 1110 that it became a royal residence when King Henry I moved in. Since then it has been used by all succeeding monarchs and can claim to be the longest-occupied palace in Europe.

Windsor Castle - Photo Courtesy of Creative Commons

Photo Courtesy of Creative Commons

Windsor Castle was originally intended to protect Norman interests on the approaches to London and a strategically important section of the River Thames. The castle was built in the traditional Norman style as a motte and bailey works, with three wards surrounding a central mound.

The original wood ramparts were replaced by Henry II – 1165 to 1179 - by massive stone walls, capable of withstanding a prolonged siege, which it did magnificently during the First Barons' War at the beginning of the 13th century.

The Crimson Drawing Room at Windsor Castle –
Photo Courtesy of Creative Commons

Henry III built a luxurious royal palace within the castle during the middle of the 13th century, and Edward III continued the works by rebuilding the palace in even grander style. Edward's grand design lasted through the Tudor period, during which Henry VIII and Elizabeth I made increasing use of the castle as a royal court and center for diplomatic entertainment.

How to Get to Windsor Castle

By Car:

Windsor Castle is about 30 miles west of Central London; take the M4 out of London to Exit 6 and then follow the signs. You'll need to plan an early visit if you would like to snag a prime parking spot.

By train:

Trains for Windsor leave roughly every 25 minutes from Paddington Station in London; the fare starts at around £8.50.

By bus:

Green Line Express Coaches routes 701 and 702 leave London's Victoria Station every 20 minutes, or so. The journey to Windsor takes about an hour and the round-trip fare is £9.

Tour Companies: Premium Tours of London operate a morning tour to Windsor Castle on Mondays, Thursdays and Saturdays with pick up at more than 170 London Hotels; Fares are: Adult 49, Children 39, and Seniors 46. The cost of the ticket includes entrance to the castle and state apartments, and the tour can be arranged through your hotel.

Admission:

Adult £18.50

Over 60/Student (with valid ID) £16.75

Under 17 £11.00

Under 5 Free

Family £48.00 (2 adults and 3 under 17s)

Admission When the State Apartments are closed

Adult £10.00

Over 60/Student (with valid ID) £9.00

Under 17 £6.50

Under 5 Free

Family £26.50 (2 adults and 3 under 17s)

You can visit for free using your London Pass

Opening Hours at Windsor Castle

March to October - 9:45am to 5:15 pm (last admission 4pm)

November to February - 9:45am to 4:15pm (last admission 3pm)

The Castle is Closed:

18 April 2014

20 April 2014 (closed until 1pm)

16 June 2014

The State Apartments are closed
13-24 January 2014

7 March 2014

5-10 April 2014

15 April 2014

And there are several days when various sections of the castle are closed too; check the 24-hour information line 1753-831118- before planning a visit.

The Cotswolds*****:

I've split the Cotswolds into two distinct and separate days out from London. You can choose the option that you think will suite you best, and then plan your day out accordingly, or you could dedicate a couple of days to the Cotswolds and see it all.

The Cotswolds Option 1

This tour takes in the Rollright Stones (a much smaller version of Stonehenge), Chipping Campden and Broadway.

The Rollright Stones

I have placed this attraction first in this section because, if you're making the trip by car, you'll probably pass by it on the way to Chipping Campden.

The Rollrights are an attraction you'll not find in many guide books. I used to visit the Rollrights when I was a child and, when they were old enough, I took my kids too. It's well worth a visit, and it's fun. Not only that, if you're driving in from London, to Chipping Campden or Broadway, you have to pass by the site, so it just makes sense to stop off along the way.

The King's Men - Copyright © Blair Howard

The Rollright Stones are part of a Neolithic site whose origins lost in the mists of time. The old legends claim that the stones once were an ancient king and his knights turned to stone by a witch. The site has three main elements: the Kings Men stone circle, the King Stone, and the Whispering Knights.

The King's Men - Copyright © Blair Howard

The Rollright Stones are, in fact, a henge. Though not as spectacular as the more famous Stonehenge, but a henge is what it is. The main circle, the King's Men, measures about 100 feet in diameter and is set on top of a small ridge just off the main road.

Now, you can believe it or not, but there is definitely a certain air of ancient mystery about this site. I remember when I used to visit that it was a very quiet spot, lacking even the sounds of the countryside – birds singing, the chirping and buzzing of insects, and so on. Well... maybe, maybe not; you'll have to judge for yourself.

One local legend has it that it's impossible to accurately count the number of stones in the circle. Maybe that's because of the numerous small stones, many of them partially hidden by the long grass and thus easily missed.

Try it, it's fun, and I bet you come up with a half dozen different counts.

The King Stone – Courtesy of Creative Commons

Just across the road from the Kings Men is the King Stone, a solitary monolith much bigger than those in the main circle. A few hundred yards further on along the path, you'll find another small group of stones, the Whispering Knights. This site once was "a turf-clad burial chamber."

The Whispering Knights – Courtesy of Brian Robert
Marshall & Creative Commons

I really do recommend you take a few moments to stop by and visit. It's interesting, fun and a great photo op.

The Rollright Stones are located right on the Oxfordshire/ Warwickshire border just off the A44 close to Long Compton. Traveling from London to Chipping Campden you'll be on the A44; watch for the signs. There's a small admission charge £1 (50p for children) which goes towards maintenance.

Chipping Campden, is the epitome of the small, Cotswold market town. Set within the Cotswold district of Gloucestershire, Chipping Campden can trace its roots all the way back to the 7th century and there's no doubt that the area was inhabited even before that during Neolithic times. In the 11th century, after the Norman conquest of England, it was recorded in King William's Domesday Book that the village had a population of 300.

In 1185, King Henry II granted a market charter to the then Lord of the manor, Hugh de Gondeville, and thus Campden became Chipping Campden, chipping being the old English word for market.

The original layout of Chipping Campden's elegant terraced High Street was designed by de Gondeville, but most of the architecture you see today dates from the 14th century to the 17th century.

In 1380, William Grevel, a local sheep merchant, and one of the richest men in England, built for himself a house on the High Street. That house, Grevel House, still stands today. The Woolstapler's Hall was built a little later by Robert Calf, another big wheel in the local wool industry.

You'll absolutely love this quaint little town. I spent many an evening frequenting one pub or the other, and many's the Saturday afternoon I rummaged through the books at the Campden Bookstore.

What to See

To walk the High Street is a singular delight. An avenue of honey-colored limestone buildings, built from the mellow locally quarried oolitic limestone known as Cotswold stone, it boasts a wealth of fine vernacular architecture. At its center stands the Market Hall with its splendid arches, built in 1627.

The Market Hall – Courtesy Creative Commons

Chipping Campden was a rich wool trading center during the Middle Ages, and enjoyed the patronage of many a wealthy wool merchant.

Today, Chipping Campden is a popular Cotswold tourist destination, and the starting point for the Cotswold Trail, a walking trail that stretches for 102 miles all the way to City of Bath. At times, especially on weekends, it can be very busy; the pubs, tea rooms, restaurants and shops especially so, but Chipping Campden is an attraction not to be missed.

Be sure to take in the grand, early perpendicular wool church of St James with its medieval altar frontals that date to the 14th century, its cope – 13th century - and its extravagant 17th century monuments to local wealthy silk merchant Sir Baptist Hicks and his family

Above you see the Church of St. James and the ruins of Campden House which was destroyed by fire during the English Civil War possibly to prevent it falling into the hands of the Parliamentarians. All that remains of this once magnificent estate are two gatehouses, two Jacobean banqueting houses, restored by the Landmark Trust, and Lady Juliana's gateway. Photo Credit: – Colin Craig and Creative Commons.

Banqueting House & St. James' Church – Courtesy W. Lloyd MacKenzie and Creative Commons

St. James' Church – Courtesy Stephen McKay and
Creative Commons

Take a quick peek at the Almshouses and Woolstaplers
Hall. The gates to Campden House and the one-time wagon
wheel wash, The Court Barn near the church is now a
museum celebrating the rich Arts and Crafts tradition of the
area.

The Alms Houses - Courtesy David Stowel and
Creative Commons

The Gates to Campden House; the old wagon wheel
wash is the depressed area at the right of the photo -
Courtesy David Stowel and Creative Commons

The Campden Bookshop in Dragon House on the High
Street has been a fascinating attraction for as long as I can

remember. The shop offers a wide selection of guide books, books on the local Arts & Crafts Movement, art, and so on; it's also a fun place to just browse.

Best Pubs:

No visit to Chipping Campden would be complete without a cool pint of beer and pub lunch. That being so, you might like to sample the fare at the delightful little Eight Bells pub on Church Street or the Kings Arms on High Street.

The Eight Bells – Courtesy Stephen McKay and Creative Commons

There are two famous and historic gardens nearby: at Hidcote Manor Garden, owned and managed by the National Trust, and at Kiftsgate, in private ownership but open to the public. Two miles to the west, in the grounds of Weston Park near Saintbury, are the earthwork remains of a motte and bailey castle.

Where to Eat

The Ebrington Arms:

An old haunt of mine, the Ebrington Arms is a country pub specializing in fine dining. Known locally for the

140

quality of its beer (very important) and for its excellent cuisine, old-world atmosphere and friendly owners – Claire and Jim Alexander – the Ebrington Arms is top of my list of places to eat. Be sure to make a reservation. 01386-593223.

The Eight Bells:

The Eight Bells, on Church Street, pictured above, is a 14th century traditional Cotswold Inn featuring a nice menu of good food offered daily for lunch and dinner. Reservations: 01386-840371

Huxley's Café and Wine Bar:

A "period Café and wine bar" on Chipping Campden's High Street is just the place for a nice lunch or an afternoon tea with fancy cakes and a cup of tea or coffee. 01386-849077

Broadway

From Chipping Campden, take the B4081 to its junction with the A-44 and drive on to the tiny Cotswold village of Broadway.

In the photo above you see Broadway's main street looking from north to south: The Swan Inn is at the left of picture as you look at it; the village green is behind the lamppost at right and you can just see the Broadway Hotel at the extreme right. This photo was taken in the mid 1960s, but it could have been taken yesterday; little has changed. Photo courtesy of Creative Commons.

Broadway claims to be the most beautiful village in England and, looking at the image on the next page, who could argue? Broadway is, perhaps, the quintessential Cotswold village.

The natural stone cottages, and elegant homes, house many of England's rich and famous. The cottages were built mostly in the early 17th century and are maintained today just as they were 300 years ago.

The photo above is a view of Broadway's main street -
Courtesy of Trevor Rickard and Creative Commons.

The Broad Way, or main street, features many antique
shops, art galleries, craft shops, pubs and tea rooms… and
it's sad to say that Broadway, over the past 50 years or so,
may have become the quintessential Cotswold tourist trap.
Prices for all things, large and small, are higher in
Broadway than almost anywhere else in the region. Be that
as it may, Broadway is a delight and a must visit, just be
careful and make sure you're getting value for money.

No visit to Broadway would be complete without a
visit to the Tower. The top of the Tower is the highest point
in the Cotswolds, and the view from the top is the best of
more than 100 such views. Even from the foot of the
Tower, the view over the Vale of Evesham is stunning;
from the top, it's unbelievable.

What to See:
Broadway Tower

Copyright © Blair Howard

The Tower was designed by James Wyatt in 1798 for the sixth Earl of Coventry, who probably had more money than sense. The Tower is built in the Norman style with three turrets and is surrounded by parkland. You can drive up the hill from Broadway, or you can hike it via a short section of the Cotswold Way: through the fields and kissing gates and over the wooden styles to the top, and then down again; it's a round-trip walk of about 5 ½ miles; allow at least three hours.

The Shops on the Broadway (actually called the High Street)

It's claimed that Broadway "has one of the longest village High Streets in the UK." I don't know if that's true, but it is quite a hike from the north end at the Swan Inn to the south end at the foot of Fish Hill. The lower high street is where you'll find all the shops, restaurants and tea shops; the upper high street offers photo ops of this quintessential Cotswold village: tiny, honey-colored cottages, some with thatched roofs, and grand old houses, all vying with one another to grow the best flower gardens, and grow them they do.

Church of St Eadburgha

The original parish church of Broadway, the Church of St Eadburgha, has been a Christian place of worship since the 12th century. The current church was built around 1400 but there are elements that remain of the original 12th century building. The dedication of a Christian church to Eadburgha is not common. Eadburgha was the grand-daughter of Alfred the Great. As a child Eadburgha was asked to choose between receiving jewels or her own Bible, she chose the Bible. The church is listed as an English Heritage Grade I English Heritage Building.

Church of St. Eadburgha – Courtesy of Creative Commons

Where to Eat

Russell's

Following on from the last entry, Russell's has, since it open a few years ago, gained a reputation as one of the finest restaurants in the area, so say my relatives and friends that visit on a regular basis. Add Russell's Fish and Chip Shop just next at Number 20a, and you have the best of both worlds.

Fish & Chips is, of course, the English staple, and Russell's serve only the finest fish. You can eat in or take away, and the shop is open for Lunch and Dinner from 12noon-2.30pm and 5.00-8.30pm, Tuesday through Saturday – closed Sunday and Monday.

The **Swan Inn** at the north end of High Street, opposite the Village Green, offers good food at reasonable prices, as does the **Broadway Hotel** at the west side of the green.

If afternoon tea is what you're craving, well… you might like to try **Tisanes Tea Rooms** at Cotswold House on the Green where, so I'm told, Tracey and Steve will provide "a nice pot of tea or coffee with cakes, sandwiches and soft drinks.

Best Pubs

Nothing is more refreshing on warm summer day that a cool pint of local beer; better yet, nothing is more refreshing than an ice-cold pint of shandy – beer and lemonade mixed together in equal parts. Broadway has several nice pubs, including the **Broadway Hotel**, the **Swan Inn** and my favorite haunt, the **Horse and Hound** on upper High Street. Another of my old haunts is the **Crown and Trumpet** on Church Street, just off the Village Green on the left. It's been a while since I was last in there, but I have a feeling it's changed very little: great pint of beer, and quiet.

This trip will take you a little father to the west visiting Burford and Bourton on the Water.

Burford

Burford is another of those historic, little market towns for which the Cotswolds are so famous. And small it is, with a population of just over 1,000, it's a sleepy town that owes it wealth and fame to the wool trade. Located just 20 miles west of Oxford on the A40, and less that 10 miles from Stow on the Wold, Bourton on the Water and Northleach, Burford is your southern gateway into the Cotswolds.

It doesn't get much nicer than this. The scene in the photo above is of Burford High Street on a sunny afternoon in winter – Courtesy of John Shortland and Creative Commons.

No one is quite sure when the area was first settled, but it seems likely that people have inhabited what is now Burford since Neolithic times. The Domesday Book, 1086, William the Conqueror's tally of his new possessions in England records a small village of approximately 200. The little community was granted a charter to hold markets either in the late 11th or early 12th Centuries, exactly when, no one seems to know.

Today, Burford is a popular stop along the way into the Cotswolds. A busy, though unspoiled little community, its businesses have a "long tradition of good service and the supply of excellent luxury and essential goods to both residents and visitors."

Sheep Street, Burford – Courtesy of Martin Bodman & Creative Commons

Burford's High Street, not so very different from its Costwold peers, is lined with the old houses and cottages so typical of the area – all built from the same honey-colored stone. Burford is timeless; a microcosm of narrow side streets and alleyways separating the 17th and 18th Century buildings. Tiny shops, tea rooms, art galleries and antiques shops offer a wealth of treasures and opportunities to enjoy that oh-so-typical English afternoon tea and cakes.

You'll also want to visit the splendid parish church, more cathedral than church, a product of the wealth that came to Burford during the era of the Cotswold wool trade

One of Burford's Alleyways – Courtesy Andy F &
Creative Commons

St John the Baptist Church, in Burford,

Wealth from wool gave the parish church of Saint John
the Baptist its current grandeur. The building was
completed in the late 1400s and its windows filled with
stained glass, of which only fragments remain. The widows
you see today are restorations carried out during the early
part of the 20th Century.

Church of John the Baptist, Burford – Courtesy of
Colin Smith & Creative Commons

The Whall Window in the Church of John the Baptist –
Courtesy of David Stowell & Creative Commons

Finally, you'll want to stroll the banks of the tiny River Windrush that meanders through the town; the same River Windrush you'll visit at Bourton on the Water.

The River Windrush at Burford – Courtesy of David Stowell & Creative Commons

Yes, Burford is, indeed, a beautiful little town. A fact that's not in dispute as Burford has been designated an Area of Outstanding Natural Beauty and is protected by the Cotswolds Conservation Board.

Burford is perfectly placed as base to explore the other famous towns and villages of the surrounding area including Oxford and Cheltenham and other attractions too.

Best Pubs:

The Mermaid Inn, Burford – Courtesy of Colin Smith
& Creative Commons

The Lamb Inn, Burford – Courtesy of Peter Watkins &
Creative Commons

Bourton-on-the-Water, one of the Cotswolds' most visited destinations, is a personal favorite of mine. I, literally, could not even hazard a guess as to how many times I've visited this quaint, old-world and visually appealing little town. My mother used to take me to Bourton when I was a small child, and I in turn would take my own children; I still visit when Bourton whenever I can.

The River Windrush - Courtesy of Keith Fairhurst and Creative Commons

Bourton-on-the-Water is just 12 miles from Burford: take the A424 to its junction with the A429 (the Fosse Way) turn left and drive on into Bourton.

Bourton-on-the-Water is named for the tiny river upon which it sits. The river Windrush is a delightful little waterway, a tinkling brook or creek that runs directly through the center of town. Along the way, a series of picturesque, low stone bridges provide access to the shops and cafes on one side of the river or the other. The riverbank is lined with trees, neatly-trimmed lawns and honey-colored Cotswold stone banks.

The River Windrush at Bourton-on-the-Water – Courtesy of Saffron Blaze and Creative Commons

All of the buildings that line the streets are built from the same honey-colored stone, most of them dating back to the 17th Century. Many of the old homes remain while others have been converted into small, intimate shops and restaurants. Bourton, today, is an important center for tourism and, sadly, perhaps a little more commercial than many of the villagers would like. Even so, the villagers do their best to make Bourton a fun place to visit

Cotswold Stone Cottages in Bourton-on-the-Water -
Courtesy of David Barnes and Creative Commons.

Bourton-on-the-Water Attractions

The main attraction, at least for me, is the river Windrush. To sit and watch the water tinkling by on warm summer afternoon is a treat; to walk the riverbanks at sunset, or even sunrise, is a rare treat, and to enjoy the waterside view along with a pint of local beer at the Old Manse pub is a treat I could not begin to describe. Try it. I think you'll agree.

Birdland

Birdland Park and Gardens, established by Len Hill, is home of some 600 species of birds, including a remarkable collection of penguins. There's also and a large pond full of fish – yes, you can feed them – the staff also present Birds of Prey and penguin feeding. It's a fun place to visit; many of the birds are allowed to fly loose among the trees.

King Penguins at Birdland Courtesy of Christine
Matthews and Creative Commons

The Model Village

The Model Village, one of the most popular of
Bourton's attractions, is located behind the Old New Inn.
The model, built by local craftsmen in the 1930s, and
opened in 1937, is an exact replica of Bourton-on-the-
Water. It's built of natural Cotswold stone to one-ninth
scale. For a small fee, you can become Gulliver for a day
and wander the streets of this miniature village at will.

The Model Village - Courtesy of Adrian Pingstone and
Creative Commons

Other attractions include a perfume factory and model railway exhibition.

Bourton is also the confluence of several long-distance walks, including the Cotswold Way, and the Heart of England Way, a 100-mile hike that actually finishes in the village.

Best Pub:

The Mousetrap Inn

With a name like that, how could it not be a great pub? Well, it is, and I can recommend it. They serve good old English "pub grub." and local English ales. Pub Grub? In this case it means they still serve the traditional Ploughman's lunch in the summer time and good hot stews and puddings in the winter. Yes, you can get a steak if you want - vegetarians are also catered for - and breakfast is available each morning; dinner is served Tuesday through Saturday.

Premier Tours out of London offer several guided tours to the Cotswolds. Go to premiertours.co.uk

This day out from London takes us northward to Shakespeare country: Stratford upon Avon and the county of Warwickshire. It's a full day out with little time to do more than hit just a few of the highlights.

Warwickshire lies at the very heart of England. In fact the tiny village of Meriden, situated between Birmingham and Coventry, claims to be the mathematical center of the nation. Be that as it may, Warwickshire offers some of the most beautiful countryside to be found anywhere in Europe.

The rolling hills and dales, and the tiny villages - some hardly more than a couple of cottages and a country store - carry on with life much as they did more than 400 years ago when the Bard of Avon strolled through the leafy glades of the great forest of Arden. The forest once covered most of Warwickshire, and although most of it is now gone, there are enough scattered fragments still remaining to remind us of what life must have been like in medieval England.

The River Avon, unspoiled and little changed from the way it must have been in Shakespeare's time, meanders southward from the ancient town of Warwick in the northeast, through the rolling countryside to Stratford-upon-Avon, then on through Bidford and Evesham until finally it links with the river Severn at Tewksbury.

It is this idyllic backdrop that was the inspiration for Shakespeare's "A Midsummer Night's Dream." Today, you can spend a quiet day lost in an atmosphere so heavy with antiquity that you can almost hear the faint voices of long ago echoing through the corridors of Warwick castle, or the tiny bedrooms of the Garrick Inn in Stratford upon Avon.

It would take the best part of a week just to visit the most popular places that lay claim to a part of

Shakespearian history. We only have a single day, so let's start in

Stratford upon Avon

The town of Stratford-Upon-Avon dates back to a time when the Bishops of Worcester ruled the area as lords of the manor. It was they who first established the popular statute fairs that are still held each year on the twelfth day of October.

William Shakespeare was born in Stratford to John Shakespeare and Mary Arden in a half-timbered Tudor house on Henly Street in 1564. The house remains today much the same as it was in Elizabethan times. The living room has a flagstone floor, white walls, and oak beams. There is a large fireplace and many fine examples of furniture of the period. Upstairs you'll find many of Shakespeare's original manuscripts, all written in old English script and flowing longhand.

Stuart Yeates and Creative Photo Courtesy of Commons

The room in which Shakespeare was born has low ceilings and windows with leaden casements. There is a large oak bed, a wooden cradle, and a fine oak chest. The windows are covered with the signatures of such famous visitors such as authors Thomas Carlyle and Sir Walter Scott.

The gardens that surround the house are beautiful indeed, and are said to contain at least one specimen of every flower, tree, and shrub mentioned in Shakespeare's plays.

The town itself has many fine restaurants and if you are hungry you could do no better than visit The Dirty Duck, The Garrick Inn, or any one of a half-a-hundred taverns and inns that specialize in the local fair of shepherd's pie, plowman's lunch, or fine sandwiches made to your order.

The Bridge over the River Avon in Stratford – Photo Courtesy of Creative Commons and Timo Newton Syms

For those who like to shop, Stratford offers the best of everything, from the local flea-market to the finest haute-couture from Paris.

Ann Hathaway's cottage, **a twelve-roomed, Elizabethan farmhouse where she lived as a child**, is located just one mile down the road in the tiny village of Shottery. Ann married Shakespeare in 1582 and the cottage remained in the Hathaway family's possession until it was acquired by the Shakespeare trust in 1892. The house contains lots of fine antique furniture, the most remarkable of which is Ann's Hathaway's bed. The rush mattress rests upon a support made from strands of rope; the exquisite needlework sheet is a Hathaway heirloom. In the living room, the lady's early willow pattern dinner service and pewter plates are displayed in a fine antique dresser. The cottage, with its orchards and delightful country garden, is open to the public all year round.

Photo Courtesy of Tony Hisgett and Creative Commons

No tour of Shakespeare's country would be complete without a visit to The Swan Theater or the Stratford

Memorial Theatre. Its terraces overlook the River Avon and offers some of the most arresting views in the area.

The Stratford Memorial Theater opened in 1932, replacing an earlier theatre built in 1879. It is here, depending on the season, that you can see such works as: Twelfth Night, Henry V, The Merry Wives Of Windsor, and A Midsummer Night's Dream, as acted out by the Royal Shakespeare Company.

Courtesy of Creative Commons and Michelle Eriksson

Before leaving Stratford you should take the time to wander through the gardens that surround the theatre, stroll along the riverbank, or linger for a moment by the Shakespeare Memorial and read the inscriptions on the statues of Hamlet, Falstaff, Prince Henry, Lady Macbeth, and Shakespeare himself.

Kenilworth and Warwick:

These two historic towns are located just a few miles to the northeast of Stratford-upon-Avon.

Kenilworth Castle:

History has seen many notable owners of Kenilworth castle: Geoffrey de Clinton in 1122, John of Gaunt, then the Earl of Leicester in 1563, and finally the Duke of Clarendon who gave it to the nation in 1958. The castle was destroyed by Oliver Cromwell during the restoration, and it has been in ruins ever since. The present ruins include

Mortimer's Tower, Leicester's Gate-House, the Great Keep, the Great Hall, and the state apartments.

The Ruins of Kenilworth Castle - Photo Courtesy of Creative Commons

The castle is open to visitors on weekdays all year round from 9.30 am until 5.30 pm and on Sundays 2pm until 5.30.

Other places of interest in Kenilworth include Latimer House, from whose steps Bishop Latimer made his last sermon before being burned at the stake in 1555, and Kenilworth's parish church, where Queen Elizabeth I worshipped when she was a guest of Lord Leicester.

The Town of Warwick;

The town of Warwick is situated only eight miles from Stratford-upon-Avon and is remarkable for its great medieval castle and cathedral-like church. The castle is unique because it is intact, having served as the home of the Earls of Warwick until the present Earl sold it 1978.

Warwick Castle:

It will take you at least half a day to tour the public rooms, galleries, and gardens of the castle. Of special interest is the great hall, the largest room in the castle. It was built in the 14th century and was the place where most of the castle activity took place.

Warwick Castle - Photo Courtesy of Creative Commons

The room is full of historical memorabilia. There's a fine collection of arms, including a full set of equestrian armor; the rider is outfitted for jousting. You will see fine paintings by Peter Paul Rubens, Anthony van Dyck, and Sir Joshua Reynolds. The magnificent shield once carried by none other than Bonnie Prince Charley hangs on the wall to the right of the central archway.

You will certainly want to visit the castle dungeon with its fine collection of instruments of torture. And you will wonder how anyone could have survived a stay in the "oubliette," a tiny dungeon within a dungeon.

If you can climb the steps to the top of the towers, you can gaze out over the countryside and imagine what brave deeds of chivalry must have taken place in the fields below.

The castle gardens are believed to be the first works of the great English gardener, Capability Brown. After you have wandered among the peacocks and taken the grand tour of the conservatory, you can take lunch or afternoon tea in the castle restaurant.

Warwick castle is open to the public all year round from 10am until 5.30 pm.

How to Get There:

Tour Groups:

Premium Tours in London offer a day trip to Warwick Castle, Stratford and Oxford: the cost is 73 for adults and the trip lasts for about 11 hours. You'll find booking info here: premiumtours.co.uk. Just log into the site and click on Out of London Tours.

By Car

Take the M40 north to junction 15 - the A429/A46 (Stratford Road) and dive on into Stratford; it's a drive of about 100 miles, motorway almost all of the way so it's an easy run.

Visit by Guided Tour

Premier Tours out of London offer several guided tours to Shakespeare Country. Go to premiertours.co.uk

Stonehenge and Salisbury*****:

Stonehenge is, arguably, THE iconic image of Britain. It's well worth a visit, but one visit will probably be enough.

Stonehenge is a prehistoric monument located in Wiltshire, about 8 miles north of Salisbury. If you're planning to do this tour on your own, I would suggest you do both Stonehenge and Salisbury.

Stonehenge is one of the most famous sites in the world, all that remains of a ring of standing stones set within a series of earthworks. I took the photo you see below more than 25 years ago; it hasn't changed much since then (joke). It's a lot less accessible today, but just as impressive.

Photo Copyright © Blair Howard

Archaeologists are unable to precisely date the monument but believe it was built sometime between 3000 BC and 2000 BC (the earthworks). Radiocarbon dating in

2008 suggested that the first stones were raised between 2400 and 2200 BC, but even that is controversial.

Salisbury:

Salisbury is a true city, not a town. In Britain, only communities with a cathedral are called cities, Salisbury has such a cathedral. Salisbury is in the county of Wiltshire, some 8 miles from Stonehenge, near the edge of Salisbury Plain at the confluence of five rivers: the Nadder, Ebble, Wylye, Avon and the Bourne, is made famous in the book, Sarum, by Edward Rutherford.

The city we know and visit today is not the original one. Back in Neolithic times it was a small settlement on the hilltop of Old Sarum. The settlement became a hill fort in the Iron Age, and then a Roman fortified camp called "Sorviodunum." When the Romans left Britain toward the end of the 4th century, Old Sarum was occupied by the Saxons, who called it "Seresberi," (close enough to "Salisbury, right?"). By 1086, in the Domesday Book, it was called "Salesberie."

Salisbury Cathedral - Photo Courtesy of Creative Commons and Mike Searle

The cathedral spire, 404 feet high, is the tallest spire in Europe.

If you visit Old Sarum (and the sight of the first cathedral), and you certainly can, you'll see how small it was, and why a new city was needed. Work began on the new city of Salisbury in 1220, with the cathedral commencing the following year. The site of the new cathedral was the site is supposed to have been selected by shooting an arrow from Old Sarum, but that cannot be true; if it was true, it would have been one heck of a shot: it's a distance of almost two miles.

I recommend making this trip by car, taking in Stonehenge, Old Sarum, Salisbury and its great cathedral.

How to Get There:

To get to Stonehenge, take the M4 west out of London to its junction with the M25; take the M25 south to its junction with the M3; take M3 west to Andover and get onto the A303 into Amesbury; Stonehenge is about a mile outside of the town. It's an easy 2-hour drive.

By Tour

Premier Tour's extended visit to Stonehenge - includes entrance fee! Go to premiertours.co.uk

Highlights:

Entrance to Stonehenge included

Audio guide tour at the site

Professional driver and luxury air-conditioned coach

Scenic drive through the Salisbury plains

The Tour:

Stonehenge

Half-day tours depart daily in the afternoons from:

1st April – 15 October 2014

Grosvenor Victoria Hotel at 1.30pm

Victoria Coach Station Gate 21 at 2:00pm

16 October 2014 – 31 March 2015

Grosvenor Victoria Hotel at 12.15pm

Victoria Coach Station Gate 21 at 12.30pm

Fare - Includes admission to Stonehenge.

Adult £31.00

Child £21.00

Senior £28.00

Where to Stay

I am not going to fill up dozens of pages with hotel reviews. There are plenty of other places that do that, and some of them specialize in London Hotels. What I will do is provide you with a half-dozen comfortable hotels I have personal knowledge of.

You'll also notice that all of the hotels listed below, with the exception of One Aldwych and the Sanctuary House, are in Victoria area. There's a very good reason for that. Victoria is easy to get to either by train, bus or Tube, and it's very easy to get to from the airports. Most of the these hotels are with a five to ten minute walk of Victoria Train and Tube stations; buses stop almost outside the front doors, and the hotels are within walking distance of the West End, the theaters, restaurants and many of London's most famous attractions.

Victoria and Belgrave Road – Courtesy of Google Maps

One Aldwych is one of London's finest, award-winning luxury hotels set in Coven Garden the heart of London, close to all the attractions. This 5-star hotel offers more than 100 luxury guest rooms and suites, a full service bar, a guest lounge and two nice restaurants: Axis at One Aldwych and Indigo. There's also a "state-of-the-art" fitness center with fully qualified personal trainers, and stunning chlorine-free swimming pool complete with underwater music. The hotel is equipped for corporate visitors with spacious eight meeting rooms and a private screening room.

The Axis Restaurant at One Aldwych, London - Photo Courtesy of Creative Commons

One Aldwych's central London location provides easy access to all of the attractions, theatres and shopping. I have stayed at this hotel and I can recommend it, always bearing in mind that things do change and it's been a while since I was there. I had no complaints; the staff was friendly and helpful; the room was luxurious and comfortable; the food was just about as good as it gets.

Rates:

The rate…from £264 per night, if you book in advance. Note: the rate is subject to change; please be sure to check online or by phone: the contact information is listed below.

Contact:

1 Aldwych, London, WC2B 4RH; Telephone: 020 7300 1000; website onealdwych.com

How to Get There:

By Tube and Mainline Train:

The nearest Tube and mainline station is Charing Cross (five minute walk); Waterloo, Covent Garden, Holborn, Temple and Chancery Lane are all just a 10 minute walk.

By Bus:

Bus Routes: 11, 13, 139, 15, 176, 23, 6, 87, 9, 91, N11, N13, N15, N155, N21, N26, N343, N44, N47, N551, N87, N89, N9, N91 all serve Covent Garden.

The Best Western Victoria Palace Hotel is just 600 yards from Victoria Train Station. I have stayed at this hotel three times. All rooms are air-conditioned with free Wi-Fi, and the front desk operates 24 hours.

The hotel is basically a no-frills establishment designed to serve visitors at a reasonable rate, and that it does. The rooms are comfortable, but typical of the Best Western Brand, and they all have air-conditioning (a real blessing in summer time), private bathrooms, satellite TV, a safe and tea and coffee-making facilities.

The Best Western Victoria Palace Hotel- Photo Courtesy of Creative Commons

Best Western Victoria Palace is just a 5-minute walk from Westminster Abbey, and 10 minutes from Buckingham Palace, Big Ben and the Houses of Parliament. The London Eye and the Royal Parks are all close by.

The main reason I stay at this hotel is its convenient location close to Victoria mainline and Tube stations. If you're arriving in London by train, this hotel will suit you nicely. It's not the best hotel in the area, but it's clean and conformatable and close to just about everything you might want to see and do: Great shopping, restaurants, art galleries and the West End are also within easy reach.

Rates:

From £122 per night.

Note: the rate is subject to change; please be sure to check online or by phone: the contact information is listed below.

Contact:

The Best Western Victoria Palace Hotel, 60-64 Warwick Way, Victoria, London SW1V 1SA, United Kingdom; Phone: 845 373 0998

How to Get There:

By Tube or Train:

The Nearest Tube and mainline station is Victoria.\

By Bus:

Bus Routes 8, 24, 38, 44, 52, 73, 82, and 185 all serve Victoria Station, which is a two minute walk from the hotel.

The Sidney Hotel London

The Sidney Hotel London on Belgrave Road in Victoria is another of those no-frills London hotels where you get exactly what you pay for: a clean and comfortable room at a good price. I have personal knowledge of this hotel and I had no complaints.

The property was extensively renovated in 2008. There are some 80 bright, modern guest rooms all with private bathrooms and 23-inch LCD TVs, breakfast - full or continental - is included in the rate which, if you're on a budget, makes the hotel even more attractive. The hotel's full-service bar serves a wide range of drinks and snacks and features a large, plasma-screen TV

The Sidney Hotel London-Victoria is a 15 minute walk from Buckingham Palace or the Royal Court Theatre. Victoria Station is just a 5 minute walk away and offers access to trains, buses, coaches and London Tube (subway) services.

Rates:

From £95 Room per night for a double room- Single, Double/Twin, Triple and Quad Rooms are available.

Note: the rate is subject to change; please be sure to check online or by phone: the contact information is listed below.

Contact:

The Sidney Hotel, 68-76 Belgrave Road, Victoria, Westminster, London, SW1V 2BP; Telephone: 020 7420 4969; From USA call toll free on 1-800-986-9403

How to Get There:

By Tube and Train

London Victoria Station is just a half-mile from the hotel.

By Bus:

The 24 bus passes the front door of the hotel every few minutes on route to Big Ben, Trafalgar Square and the West End.

The Holiday Inn Express London-Victoria on bustling Belgrave Road is within easy walking distance of major attractions: Westminster Abbey, Buckingham Palace; , Oxford Street and the shops; and the Houses of Parliament are close enough for you to hear Big Ben chime; the London Eye is just a few minutes away.

There's not too much to say about this hotel, but what I can say is all good. I've stayed there several times and have never had a bad experience. The rooms are typical of the brand: nice, clean, with all the amenities, including free ireless Internet, private bathrooms, etc. Complimentary buffet breakfast is available and in the evening you can relax in the hotel bar; the staff is friendly and helpful.

Rates:

From £135 Room per night for a double room.

Note: Rate is subject to change; please be sure to check online or by phone: the contact information is listed below.

Contact:

Holiday Inn Express - London Victoria Hotel, 106-110 Belgrave Road, London, SW1V 2BJ England; 1 877 865 6578

How to Get There:

Because of its close proximity Victoria train and Tube stations, getting to Holiday Inn Express London-Victoria is easy. Heathrow Airport is quickly and easily accessible by Tube from Victoria station; Gatwick Airport is just a short express train ride away, also via Victoria station.

By Tube:

The nearest Tube Station is Pimlico, with Victoria only a couple of minutes more away.

By Bus:

The 24 bus passes the front door of the hotel every few minutes on route to Big Ben, Trafalgar Square and the West End.

Sanctuary House,

Sanctuary House Hotel, Westminster

I have only stayed at the Sanctuary House once, but I was impressed nevertheless. The Sanctuary House is located one of London's oldest and most fashionable areas, just a short walk from Westminster Abbey and Houses of Parliament and all of the other attractions.

This is a Fuller's brand hotel with some 34 rooms, all individually decorated, comfortable and clean. The Fuller's pub on the first floor is welcoming and serves home-cooked food with a full range of fine wines and beer available. The pub is the one thing about this hotel that I remember most. The staff is friendly and always ready to help with bookings and directions.

The Sanctuary House is a 10-minute walk from St James's Park, with The Mall and St James's Palace. Oxford and Regent Streets are about a mile away.

Rates:

From £160 per night.

Note: Rates are always subject to change; please be sure to check online or by phone: the contact information is listed below.

Contact:

The Sanctuary House Hotel, 33 Tothill Street, Westminster, London, SW1H 9LA , 020 7799 4044

How to Get There:

By Tube:

The nearest Tube station is St. James' Park

By Bus:

Bus Routes 11, 24, 148 and 211 all serve the Sanctuary house

Comfort Inn Victoria

Finally, we come to the Comfort Inn Victoria located in the prestigious Royal Borough of Westminster. The hotel is a renovated Georgian Town House now offering 48 guest rooms, all with air-conditioning and private bathrooms (showers only) and, if you like to do for yourself, there are several rooms with a kitchenette and microwave for self-catering. The Comfort Inn also serves a nice breakfast and the front desk is open 24 hours a day.

The hotel is located close to Central London, and Heathrow Airport is quickly and easily accessible by Tube from Victoria station; Gatwick Airport is just a short express train ride away, also via Victoria station. Westminster Abbey, Buckingham Palace; Oxford Street and the shops, the Houses of Parliament and the London Eye is just a few minutes away by bus or Tube.

Rates:

From £144 per night

Note: Rates are always subject to change; please be sure to check online or by phone: the contact information is listed below.

Contact:

The Comfort Inn Victoria, 18-24 Belgrave Road, Victoria, London, SW1V 1QF, United Kingdom; + 44 (0) 20 7233 6636; Fax: + 44 (0) 20 7932 0538

How to Get There:

By Tube:

Victoria Train and Bus Stations are just a short five minute walk away.

By Bus:

Bus Routes 11, 24, 148 and 211 all serve the Comfort Inn Victoria

Where to Eat

Again, there are literally thousands of restaurants in London. It would take a lifetime, and then some, to visit them all. I have dined at dozens of London restaurants: some of them good, some of them bad, some of them really bad. And, as we all know, restaurants come and go at an alarming rate: restaurants we visited yesterday are gone tomorrow. With all of that in mind, I am not going to load you up with a long list of restaurants. I am including only a few tried and trusted restaurants of which I have personal experience: restaurants I know you will enjoy.

Rules – Covent Garden

Rules is the oldest restaurant in London. It was established in 1798 by Thomas Rules, and specializes in "traditional British food." I've eaten at Rules a couple times. If you like gamey food, this is the place for you. The cuisine includes the likes of fresh oysters, game pies, and puddings; pheasant, partridge, wild duck, hare, assorted steaks, fish, roe deer, and the house specialty, Belted Galloway beef.

Photo Courtesy if Creative Commons

The dress code is "smart casual" - coats and ties are not required. You will need to make a reservation, and you better do it in advance; this is a popular restaurant. Be prepared to dig deep into your wallet; a typical dinner for two will set you back £120, give or take, and that does not include drinks.

So, what's it like? As I said, if you like game, this is the place for you; I don't particularly like it, so I tend to stick with either steak or fish – the halibut is very nice. I also like fresh oysters, but at £2.50 each I tend not to indulge, unless it's a special occasion. They serve a nice pint of bitter too. All-in-all, I don't think you'll be disappointed, and it is a rather grand experience.

Contact:

Rules, 35 Maiden Lane, Covent Garden, London, WC2E ; Telephone: 020 7836 5314; website rules.co.uk

How to Get There:

Nearest Tube Stations: Leicester Square, Covent Garden, Charing Cross,

By Bus:

Buses Routes 6, 9, 11, 13, 15, 23, 24, 29, 87, 91, 139, 176 all serve Covent Garden

Porter's English Restaurant

Porter's English Restaurant is also in Covent Garden. I have eaten at Porters maybe a half-dozen time; it's one of the restaurants I try to visit each time I'm in London. Porter's was opened by the Earl of Bradford in 1979. He wanted to provide good English food at a price everyone could afford. He certainly managed to do that, and the prices are just as affordable today as they were back then, and the food is excellent.

Porters English Restaurant in Covent Garden is very child friendly. Children have their own menu and cocktail list!

My recommendations: Porters Steak and Kidney Pudding is about as good as it gets, the Fisherman's Pie is my all-time favorite; and Beer Battered Cod, another of my favorites, is a cod fillet deep fried; served with tartar sauce.

You can eat at Porter's for less than 20 per person (at least 20 entrees cost less than £14), or you can spend as much as £75 per person. Here are a few items that will get the juices flowing: Steak, Guinness and Mushroom Pie £12.85; Mince Beef, Onion, Pea and Red Wine Pie £12.85;

Steak and Cheddar Pie £12.85; Fisherman's Pie £12.85 (one of my favorites: Cod, salmon and prawns, in a creamy dill and parsley sauce with creamy mashed potato and cheddar cheese topping); Braised Lamb Shank Pie £13.95; Shepherd's Pie £12.85. Steak and Kidney Pudding £12.95.

Note: While the prices quoted were current at the time of writing, they are always subject to change.

Reservations are a must

Contact:

Porters English Restaurant, 17 Henrietta Street, Covent Garden, London, WC2E 8QH; Telephone: 020 7836 6466

Website: porters.uk.com

How to Get There:

Nearest Tube Stations: Leicester Square, Covent Garden, Charing Cross,

By Bus:

Buses Routes 6, 9, 11, 13, 15, 23, 24, 29, 87, 91, 139, 176 all serve Covent Garden

Simpson's-in-the-Strand:

Simpson's-in-the-Strand is an upscale establishment and something of a landmark. Simpson's has been serving "classic British cuisine" for more than 170 years, including the best Roast Beef that I have ever tasted, and the Lamb is just as good.

My recommendation: Try Simpson's signature Roast rib of Scottish beef (aged 28 days) served with roast potatoes, savoy cabbage and, of course, Yorkshire pudding and horseradish sauce.

Roasts are brought to your table on antique silver-domed carts and carved, on-the-spot by one of Simpson's Master Carvers.

Simpson's is not astronomically expensive, but you can expect to spend 50 or 60 per person, without drinks.

Reservations are a must

Dress Code: Smart casual, no jeans, tee shirts, etc.

Address:

Simpson's-in-the-Strand

100 Strand
London
WC2R 0EW
Telephone:

020 7836 9112
Official Website:

www.simpsonsinthestrand.co.uk

Le Pont De La Tour:

Le Pont De La Tour is on the embankment overlooking Tower Bridge; it's just the perfect spot for lunch during your visit to the Tower of London.

For dinner, it's even better. To sit and dine on the Terrace with Tower Bridge all in lights is a really memorable experience.

My recommendation: I suggest you try the Braised Lamb shank with pommes purée; if you like lamb, you'll love it.

What does it cost? Well, you can certainly eat for less, but I'm not sure you can get better value for money, especially considering the location. Expect to pay 100 and up for dinner for two.

Reservations for dinner are a must

Address: Butlers Wharf, 36d Shad Thames, London SE1 2YE; Telephone: 020 7403 8403

How to Get There:

By Tube

Nearest Tube Station: London Bridge

By Bus:

Routes: RV1, 17, 21, 35, 40, 43, 47, 133, 141, 149, 343, 381, 521 (or any **bus** to London Bridge) all serve London Bridge

Opening Times:

Restaurant

Lunch: Mon - Sun 12pm-3pm

Dinner: Mon - Sun 6pm - 11pm

(Sunday - closes 10.30pm)

Bar & Grill

Lunch: Mon - Fri 12pm-3pm

Dinner: Mon - Fri 6pm - 11pm

Saturday - open all day: 12pm-11pm

Sunday - open all day: 12pm-10.30pm

Official Website: www.lepontdelatour.co.uk

Dress Code:

Restaurant: Smart dress

Bar & Grill: Casual dress

So there you have it, the London you've read about and now plan to visit. I hope you enjoy your time in England's first city as much as I always do, and I hope this book will help to make your visit and amazing and memorable experience.

Oh, by the way, just to follow up on the day trips to the Cotswolds, Stratford, Warwick, etc., I have also written guide books to those areas too: you might want to grab a copy of those books too. You'll find the links on the next page.

Thank You:

I sincerely hope you enjoyed this book. Thank you so much for downloading it.

If you have comments of questions, you can contact me by email at blair@blairhoward.com. I will reply to all emails. And you can also visit my website www.blairhoward.com for a complete list of my books.

If you enjoyed the book, I would really appreciate it if you could take a few moments and share your thoughts by posting a review on Amazon.

Other Books by this Author:

The Visitor's Guide to the English Cotswolds

Visitor's Guide to Shakespeare Country